THIS IS SURFBOARD SAILING

REINHART WINKLER

First published © 1979
by
United Nautical Publishers SA, Basle

This edition published © 1979
by
NAUTICAL PUBLISHING COMPANY LTD
Nautical House, Lymington, Hampshire, England

in association with
George G. Harrap & Co Ltd
London

ISBN 0 245 53449 0

No part of this book or its
illustrations may be reproduced
without permission of
United Nautical Publishers SA

Text setting by: BAS Printers Limited, Over Wallop, England
Printing by: New Interlitho, Trezzano, Italy

Part 2. Continued

Surf-sailing	168
The behaviour of waves	169
Surfing and surf-sailing	170
Surf-sailing in tidal waters	172
Special equipment	173
Safety when surf-sailing	175
Working out through the breakers	176
Starting in the water	176
Racing start	177
Off-the-beach start	180
Surf-sailing against the waves	180
Tacking against the waves	182
Leaping off the waves	182
Foot straps	184
Waiting and resting	185
Surf-sailing on the waves	185
The ten safety rules for surf-sailing	186

Racing	188
How to sail the course	191
The windward leg	192
The reaching leg	192

Other types of competiton	194
Team racing	194
Slalom	194
Surf racing	195
Buoy ball	196

Freestyle boardsailing	197
Sailing to leeward	198
Inside the boom	198
Boardsailing backwards	198
Helicopter or 360° turn	198
Pirouette	199
Sailing lying down	199
Rail-riding	199
Backwards somersault	199

Tandem sailboards	200

Boardsailing on ice	205

Boardsailing on land	207

Part 2. Advanced boardsailing — 101

Basic technique in strong winds	102
The force 4 hurdle	104
Mast to windward	104
Raising the sail	106
Balance	107
Co-ordination of movement	107
Ready for take-off	110
Sheeting in gradually	112

Boardsailing in a strong wind—speed madness	117
Finer points of strong wind technique	120
Gusty winds	121
Planing	122
Dangers in strong winds	124
Safety rules at sea	125

Special hard weather gear	127
Sails	127
Storm sails	127
Storm sail with shortened luff	128
The all-weather or all-round sail	129
Making storm sails	130
Harnesses	131
The Hawaii harness	132
The Charchulla Channel system	132
Sailorsurf adjustable hook	133
Sailorsurf moulded rubber glove/hooks	133
The daggerboard	134
Storm daggerboard	134
Centreboard	137

Courses in strong winds	138
Close-hauled	138
Beam reaching and broad reaching	140
Running	141

Tacking and gybing in strong winds	144
Tacking	144
A jet tack	146
A duck tack	146
Gybing	148
Running or catapult gybe	148
Stop gybe	150

Strong-wind falls	152
Diving falls	154
Windward flop	154
Catapult fall	154
Capsize fall	155

Boardsailing without a daggerboard	159
The skeg	161

Body dip and head dip	162

The water start	166

Contents

Part 1. Boardsailing for beginners — 3

Gear and equipment — 4

The sailboard — 4
The board itself — 6
   Hints on repairs — 8
The rig — 8
   The universal joint — 9
   The mast — 9
   The wishbone boom — 9
   The sail — 10
The skeg or fin — 12
The daggerboard — 12
Rigging the sailboard — 13
   Knots — 14
Transport — 18
Tools and spares — 19
Clothing — 20
   Shoes — 20
   Gloves — 21

Boardsailing for beginners — 23

Where to learn — 24
The wind and sailing area — 25
Balancing the rig — 27
Practising on land — 28
Balancing the board — 33
Paddling — 34
Towing — 35
Raising the sail — 35
Lifting the sail to windward — 39
Turning — 39
Getting under way — 43
Sailing straight — 47
Luffing up and bearing away — 54
Running before the wind — 58
The sailing terms — 60
Head to wind — 60
Close-hauled — 60
Sailing to windward — 60
Beam reach — 61
Broad reach — 61
Running — 61
Changing tacks — 62
Gybing — 66
Sailing round a circle — 70
Falling — 72
Relaxation — 73

The theory of sailing — 75

Sail power by push — 76
Sail power by pull — 76
Camber — 79
Angle of attack — 80
Steering a sailboard — 80
Adjustment of sail camber — 83

The weather — 86

Highs, lows and wind — 87
Land and sea breezes — 88
Thunderstorms — 92

Safety — 94

The boardsailor's safety rules — 95
Long distance boardsailing rules — 96
Right-of-way rules — 97
Personal buoyancy aids — 97
Restrictions — 98

Foreword

I simply can't explain how the idea of combining a wishbone-boom and a universal joint occurred to me as the way to steer and control a board and sail while standing up. No inventor could. All I can say is that in May of 1967 while driving on the San Bernardino Freeway just outside Los Angeles, the notion gradually took form.

By the time I reached home I was pretty sure it was the answer . . . To what? . . . To the simplest possible sailing machine where the sailor directly involves himself in the dynamics of the craft. One board, one sail, one boom, a mast, a joint, a few strings and that's it.

Why wasn't it invented before? One reason is technical, namely, that the materials have only recently become available. A windsurfer built in, say, 1930, would weigh about 100 to 150 pounds because there was neither fibreglass reinforced plastic nor polyester foam nor dacron sailcloth. A board this heavy would have been sluggish and slow and would have appealed only to a few rugged individualists. It wasn't until 1960 that a windsurfer could be built weighing the 60 or so pounds it does today. Even then it might not have been invented, and certainly wouldn't have flourished were it not for certain special social and psychological conditions.

50 years ago the only sensible reason to go near water was mercantile, that is, to make money. In Europe, and most of North America, there was simply no time and no reward for imagining such foolishness as windsurfing. Today, however, it is considered acceptable, even heroic, to challenge ski slopes, rock faces and water ski tow lines during our increasing amount of spare time. To put it another way, the concept of holding the wind in your hands, crashing through mountains of waves and down canyons of surf became absolutely irresistible to western man . . . once he had nothing better to do.

I am really surprised that the windsurfing sport has progressed so far so quickly. The size of the following, about a quarter of a million people, is truly astonishing. Not only that, board design and construction, riding techniques and professional instruction have all improved dramatically since that day in July 1967 when I had to teach myself how for the first time ever. This book collects everything that is known today, 12 years later, about surfboard sailing. It will show you how, beginning in light winds and flat water, all the way through to the thrills of heavy wind surfing in tall waves. Along the way it will illustrate the tricks and techniques developed and used by world class windsurfers. All in all it will complement and enhance your windsurfing experience.

James R. Drake, inventor of the Windsurfer

Reinhart Winkler

Part 1 BOARDSAILING FOR BEGINNERS

Gear and equipment

The sailboard

There is your board, lying on the beach for the first time, looking sleek and beautiful—a product of modern technology and shaped to perfection; it curves slightly along its length, the bow points up a little and the sides are rounded with no sharp corners or projections. Experts consider it to be the simplest and most beautiful of sailing craft.

It is hard to believe that you will soon skim over the water as elegantly and effortlessly as the boardsailors that you have hitherto only been able to watch enviously and incredulously. But, even for a beginner, it is not so very difficult provided that you bear a few points in mind:

- You need to know what material has been used and how your sailboard has been made if you are to be able to handle it properly. Do not throw away the instructions on assembly and use, but take them home to study quietly for an hour.
- Later on, when you have tried and fallen in a time or two, do not give up until the boardsailing germ has taken a firm hold. Once you have caught the bug properly the fever will run its course automatically, as do all infectious diseases, and you will soon learn how to boardsail.

As a beginner it does not matter what type of sailboard you use when learning; the fine distinctions between the various makes can, in any case, only be appreciated by those with more experience. Unlike sailing boats the proven rule is that technique is all-important; the type of sailboard matters relatively little, even when sailboard racing. Naturally your sailboard must function properly, but if something goes wrong during your first attempts do not think disappointedly—why didn't I buy that other make of sailboard—I wish I had spent a little more—if only . . . ! The basic techniques can be learnt on any board.

Above: Modern technology and the simplest of sailing systems are responsible for these beautifully shaped plastic boards.

Right: There are well over 100 different types of sailboard sold in Europe today and the differences between them are often very small. The great sport of boardsailing can be learnt on any make of board.

The board itself

Most of the boards available today are about 3·60 m (11 ft 7 ins) in length, 60–70 cm (2 ft–2 ft 3 ins) wide and weigh 22–26 kg (48–57 lbs), exclusive of mast and sail but complete with dagger-board. A volume of roughly 250 litres (9 cubic feet) provides adequate buoyancy for boardsailors of normal weight. Only very heavy people who weigh more than 85–90 kg (13–14 stone or 185–200 lbs) will find it difficult to get a light board to plane.

Although the sailboard is longer it is very similar in shape to the surfboards that have been used for many years by surfers, and not unlike those used on busy beaches by lifeguards when rescuing swimmers who have been swept out to sea.

Most sailboards are made either of polyethylene or GRP (glass-fibre reinforced plastics). These materials are moulded to form a shell which covers and protects the inner core which is a rigid plastic foam. It is this foam that ensures that the board is stiff and will float and support a sailor, even when it has been badly damaged. Later on, if you get blown far from the land when boardsailing in strong winds or surf, never forget that your board *always* floats and will *always* support you, acting as a life raft.

Polyethylene is a rather soft plastic with a matt surface. A tubular sheath of polyethylene sheet about 2 mm (·08 in) thick is filled with foam in a pressure mould. Slight surface indentation is a sign of a second quality board, but it will still function satisfactorily. A polyethylene board left

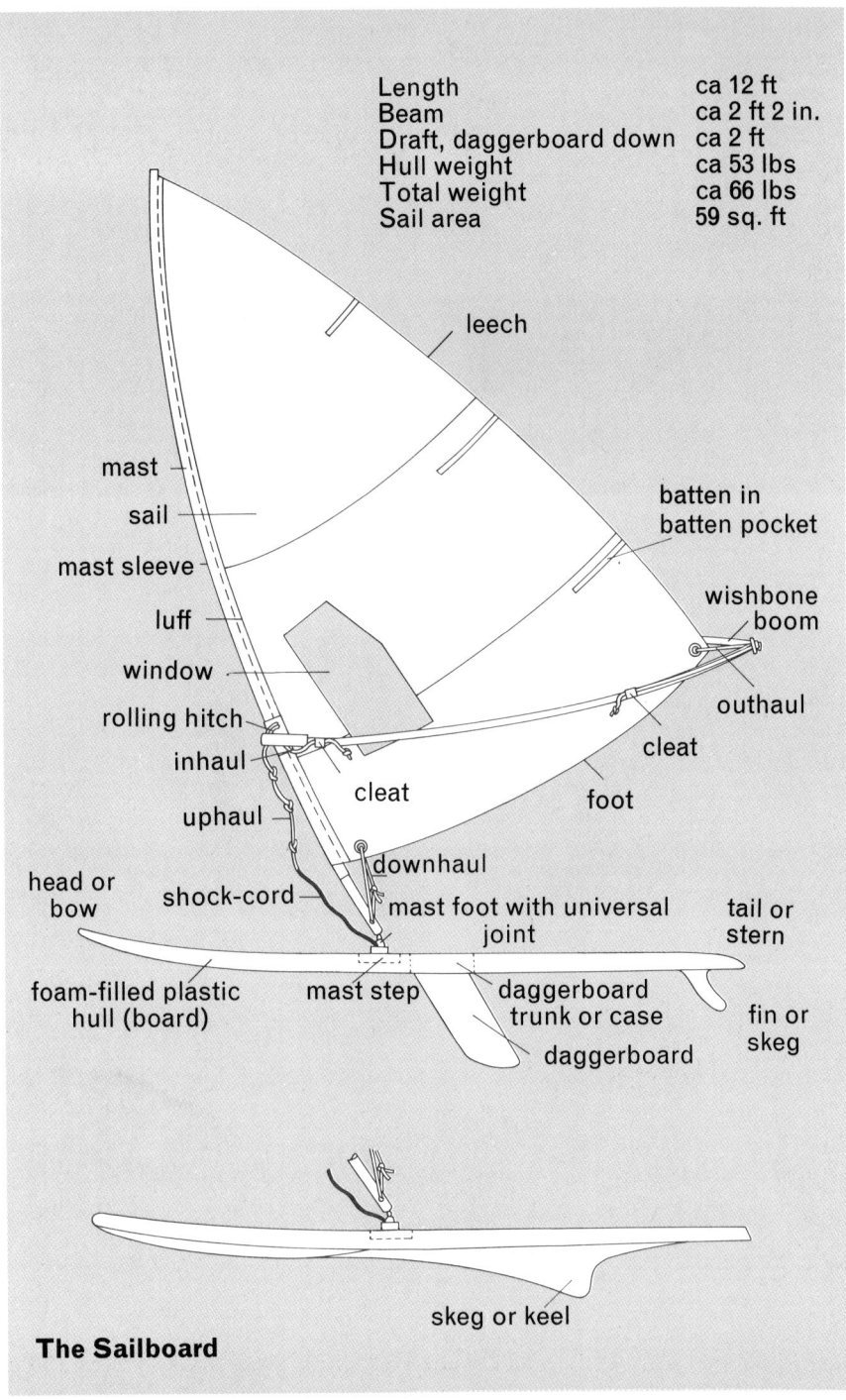

Length	ca 12 ft
Beam	ca 2 ft 2 in.
Draft, daggerboard down	ca 2 ft
Hull weight	ca 53 lbs
Total weight	ca 66 lbs
Sail area	59 sq. ft

The Sailboard

lying on the sand in very bright sunshine can become distorted because the material is rather sensitive to heat; on the other hand minor damage can easily be repaired with a soldering iron.

The surface and structure of GRP boards are always hard. The shell is a laminate of glass-fibre filaments impregnated with synthetic resin. A particularly tough but thin layer of polyester resin, the gelcoat, protects the laminate from the harmful action of water. After a period of hard use it is quite normal for fine hair cracks to appear in the gelcoat. GRP boards are generally less flexible, and do not give to the waves as much as polyethylene boards.

Although experts argue over the advantages and disadvantages of the different materials they are unanimous on one point: a boardsailor must always have a non-slip surface on which to stand! This is a much more active sport than normal sailing; the fastest board is useless and the best of winds is wasted if you keep slipping off. Good shoes, even those designed especially for boardsailing, do not help much. GRP boards with their high-gloss finish are usually roughened where you stand, but this roughness is often too sharp initially and then wears smooth in time. Falling on the roughened area can cause grazed elbows and knees. What can be done?

Boardsailing is an active sport. The surface on which you stand must be really non-slip because a boardsailor has only his feet to provide grip.

- Wash down a brand new board with hot water, or even with petrol, to remove any parting agent that may remain after manufacture.
- Roughen the standing area of GRP boards carefully with abrasive paper, but be careful not to remove the gelcoat and so lay bare the laminate beneath.
- Stick strips of adhesive tape, with a non-slip backing such as fine sand, along the standing area lengthwise and 10 cm (4 ins) apart. This is only a short-term solution.
- The best method is to clean the standing area carefully and then apply wax. Special wax aerosols can be bought from most surf-shops, but ordinary beeswax is good too and will give a non-slip matt surface on which bare feet can get a good hold. The wax has to be renewed from time to time and will, of course, attract dirt.

Hints on repairs

Like most plastic products sailboards require little maintenance; an occasional wash-down with soap or a special cleaner is quite adequate. If you have been on a beach where there are patches of oil or tar you can remove the marks easily with petrol.

Never forget that the outer shell of all types of board is very thin and vulnerable. It can easily be dented or cracked if you hit a sharp corner, for example when putting it on the roof-rack or when putting it down on a sharp stone. Water should never be allowed to penetrate to the foam inside; even closed-cell foam can absorb water, become less buoyant and deteriorate in time, particularly when attacked by sea water or frost.

If the surface alone is damaged a GRP board can be repaired using the filler supplied with GRP packs. First clean the area thoroughly with petrol or acetone so that the filler is able to stick firmly to a grease-free surface. When the filler has hardened complete the repair by rubbing down, first with medium-grade abrasive paper and then with fine, so that it is absolutely smooth and faired into the shell. Take care not to damage the surrounding gelcoat. The repair will be almost invisible if you use polyester resin of the same colour as your board instead of filler.

A hole that penetrates to the foam core inside is more difficult to deal with but can be repaired. First clean up the edges of the hole with a pad saw, sand them smooth and remove dirt and grease as described above. Then fill the hole with patches of glassfibre mat, cut to shape, and impregnate them thoroughly with polyester resin, dabbing this well in with a hard paint brush to remove any air bubbles in the glass mat. It does not matter if the patches overlap the edges of the hole initially, but they must be sanded off after the repair has cured. A final gelcoat of (coloured) polyester resin is essential. You can get a completely smooth and level surface by rubbing down with fine paper, preferably wet, and then by covering the area with transparent film, well smoothed down, while the gelcoat is still tacky.

The daggerboard trunk can be damaged if the daggerboard is lifted out too late when running the sailboard up onto a beach. This is difficult to repair because, generally, part of the heavily-stressed load-bearing structure of the board will be crushed. Filling or patching is ineffective and it is best to take your board to an expert at the nearest sailboard agency.

Repairing surface damage to polyethylene boards is much simpler, Scratches or deeper scars can be dealt with easily with a soldering iron. You can buy sheets of polyethylene of varying thickness, or small rolls of round, wire-like polyethylene, rather like solder. A deeper hole should first be filled with putty and the sheet of polyethylene is then welded over it to give a smooth surface.

GRP cannot be used to repair polyethylene boards, nor vice versa.

Apart from the board itself a complete sailboard has three other components: the rig including the sail, which provides the power: the daggerboard, which discourages sideways motion when sailing to windward: the skeg, which helps steering and provides directional stability.

The rig

The rig consists of the mast with its jointed mast foot, the boom and the sail. The mast foot is unique to sailboards because it incorporates a universal joint which allows the mast to tilt and turn in all directions. No other sailing craft have masts of this type. Sailings boats often have very tall masts that have to be supported on all sides by taut wires called stays and shrouds. Most small sailing dinghies have stayed masts, although some, such as the well-known Olympic single-hander, the Finn, have unstayed masts, but these are held rigidly upright and only pivot about a vertical axis when the sail is eased out and pulled in to suit the wind and the boat's course. Absolute freedom to tilt or turn in any direction is the essential characteristic of the sailboard rig and is the essential key to sailboarding techniques, including sailing in breaking surf and performing freestyle tricks.

The universal joint

Although there are already more than a hundred varieties of sailboards there are two basic types of mast joints:

Mechanical: steel or hard moulded nylon.

Structural: flexible solid rubber.
There is a greater risk of breaking a stainless steel mechanical joint, but the more important disadvantage is that the boardsailor is more likely to injure his foot on it than on a rubber joint. The mast foot itself, beneath the joint, connects the mast firmly to the board and is usually some form of peg or tenon which fits into the mast step. This step is a matching aperture in the board. The mast foot is held into the step by a variety of methods.

The mast foot has to stay firmly connected to the board, for example it must not become disengaged when the sail is raised up out of the water. On the other hand it should be capable of being released sufficiently easily to avoid any danger of injuring a foot or a leg. The more progressive manufacturers have therefore developed an adjustable release device so that the mast is automatically released from the board when a certain load comes onto it.

Always keep the mast foot and step clean and free of sand so that they fit together perfectly.

The mast

Masts are made either of aluminium or of GRP. Although aluminium withstands bumps and blows better it is less flexible because it is not usually tapered and the material is harder. In a hard wind it is not possible to flatten the sail to the same extent. Aluminium masts are also more likely to break and they have not proved so successful although some manufacturers have tried using high strength alloys.

A GRP mast is made up of many thin laminates of glass-fibre cloth, wound spirally to produce the tapering conical shape which gives it the exceptional flexibility that has not yet been matched by an aluminium mast. This is extremely important because it is the shape built into the sail, that is its camber, that produces the driving force. The right camber, flat for strong winds and full for light breezes, can only be obtained and varied to match the strength of the wind if the mast is sufficiently flexible.

Never forget that the surface of the mast is extremely vulnerable and so be careful not to bump or bang it when you are carrying or storing it.

The wishbone boom

Like the mast joint this is a characteristic feature of sailboards. The mast and boom together keep the sail extended.

You use the boom to hold the rig upright and to steer the sailboard, but at the same time you support yourself by it, and it is therefore vital that it should be light in weight and easy to grasp. Whether it is made of

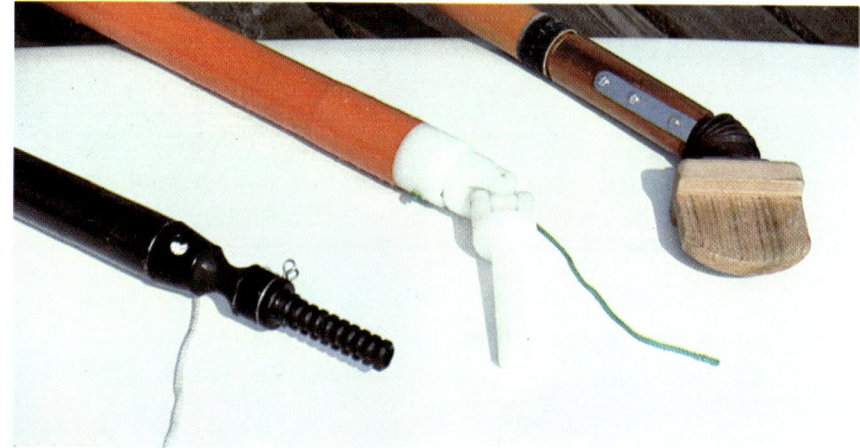

The mast foot joint is the vital part of all sailboards. Because it is a universal joint the mast can be moved in any direction. Left, moulded flexible rubber. Right, two mechanical joints, the centre joint is solid nylon, the one on the right is stainless steel which here is covered by a rubber sleeve which protects the boardsailor's foot from injury.

wood or of aluminium the critical point about a wishbone boom is how much it flexes. It has to be sufficiently rigid to withstand the loads that are put on it in gusts and strong winds. If it is too flexible it will splay out more as the boardsailor puts his weight on it when pressure on the sail increases. This causes the sail to become fuller, particularly on a close-hauled course, which is just when a full sail is least desirable. The stiffer the wishbone boom the better will be the close-hauled performance.

There are certain disadvantages to a wooden boom, as compared to aluminium. Although wood provides a good hand-hold it weighs more and this makes it harder to hold the rig up. An aluminium boom must be foam-filled to prevent water entering because the rig has to be buoyant. A buffer at the forward end is needed to avoid damaging the board when the rig falls, and it is preferable to have a second buffer at the aft end as well. Some booms have a protective covering material, others are bound with rubber, leather or cloth tape. If your boom is completely bare you should at the very least strap adhesive cloth tape round it where your hands grasp it, but you will have to renew the tape from time to time.

The sail

Although the sailboard itself is a brand new type of sailing craft the sail has been adopted unchanged from conventional sailing boats. Obviously the source of power is the same, the wind, and its energy is transmitted by the same engine, the

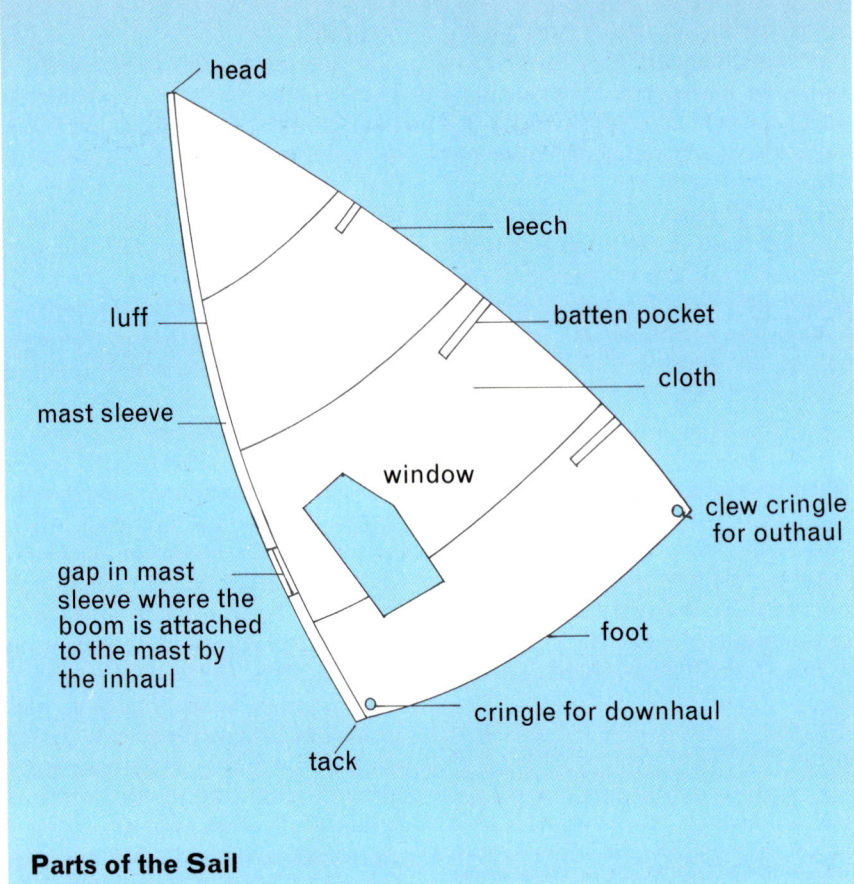

Parts of the Sail

sail. The differences from the conventional rig are small in that the sailboard's sail has a sleeve which is just pulled over the mast, and it also has a loose foot. The sail is still triangular in shape and the material of which it is made is the same, synthetic rot-proof fibre. Sails should have large windows fitted so that the boardsailor can see clearly in all directions.

The area of a normal sail is generally about 5·50 m² (59 sq ft). Instead of reducing the area in strong winds by reefing, a smaller sail is used, such as the 4·50 m² (48 sq ft) all-weather, or all-round, sail which is cut specifically for use when the wind strength increases. The 3·50 m² (37 sq ft) storm sail is designed for really hard winds but can also be used by children or by learners when the wind is moderate. There are also extra-large sails of 6·50 m² (70 sq ft) for use when racing and in light weather, but size has to be limited by the length of the boom.

Those sails that are cut with a rounded convex leech have battens to support the trailing edge; these are

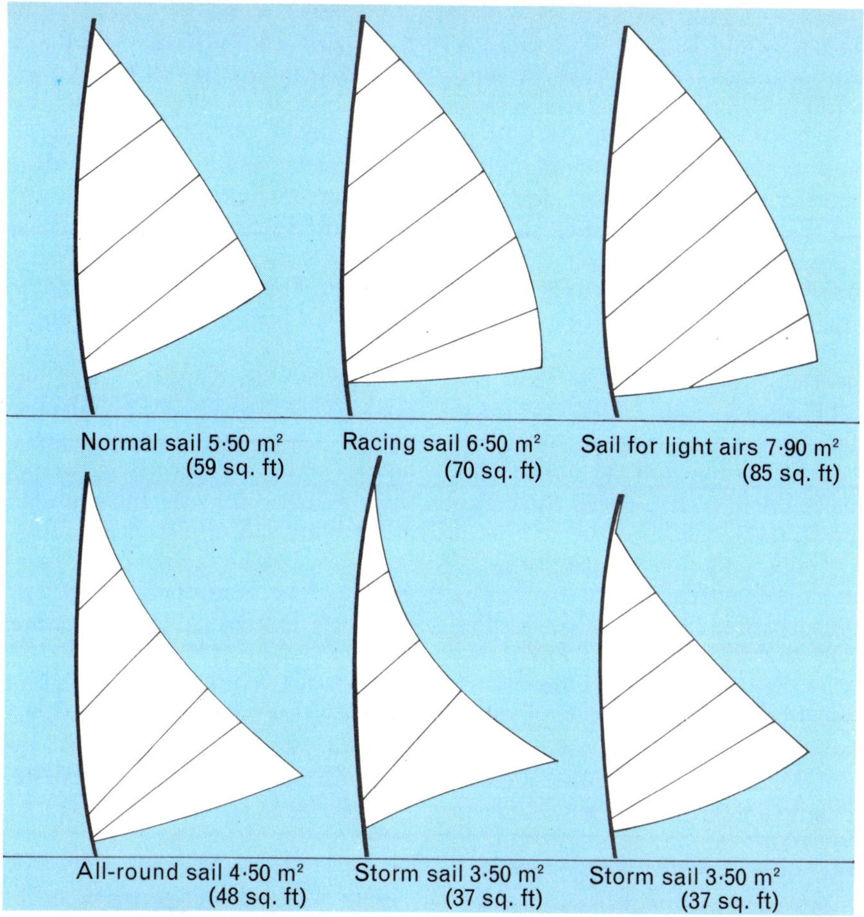

Normal sail 5·50 m² (59 sq. ft)
Racing sail 6·50 m² (70 sq. ft)
Sail for light airs 7·90 m² (85 sq. ft)
All-round sail 4·50 m² (48 sq. ft)
Storm sail 3·50 m² (37 sq. ft)
Storm sail 3·50 m² (37 sq. ft)

The various sailboard sails.

This is how to fold up the sail. Work from the foot upwards, folding the sail back and forth parallel to the seam so that the mast sleeve lies in a zig-zag. Then fold it lengthwise into a neat packet.

inserted into pockets sewn onto the sail.

A sailboard's sail is subjected to much greater wear than those of other sailing craft because it is so often dropped into the water and also gets such rough treatment on the beach. As a beginner your sail will undoubtedly be in the water more often than not and, although this is quite normal, you should make amends by looking after it carefully. Today all sails are made of synthetic fibres with a smooth surface which offers little resistance to the wind. They hold their shape well and do not rot. Coloured sails are generally just as durable as white.

After an outing you could just stuff your soaking wet sail away in its sailbag but—a little care pays handsomely. Dry it first, extended on the mast and the boom, for a couple of minutes, and shake off any sand and mud.

If you are fairly close to home there is no need to dismantle the rig completely. Just release the outhaul, roll the sail round the mast, fold the boom up to the mast and lash it tight into a neat package ready to go on your roof-rack. The great advantage of doing this is that your boom is already attached to the mast next time you go out, and it will take barely a minute to assemble the rig ready to go for a sail. If you have a longer drive home it is better to take the rig completely to pieces. Remove the sail but do not fold it like a table cloth or roll it up; fold it along the seams working up from the foot with the mast sleeve zig-zagging on top. Then fold up or roll up the resulting long sausage.

Inspect your sail regularly for signs of wear and damage. The seams are particularly likely to go by the batten pockets, the cringles may start to pull out, or a stone could have made a small tear. Adhesive tape is often quite adequate for minor repairs.

Any damage to batten pockets, larger tears, or cringles that have pulled out should be properly repaired, and at once, because otherwise the sail will soon become unusable and this could spoil your whole weekend.

The skeg or fin

The large mahogany surfboards used by the kings of Hawaii centuries ago weighed a good 50 kg (110 lbs) and had neither skegs nor daggerboards. It was not until 1935, by which time surfing had become an established sport in Hawaii, that the American Tom Blake hit on the idea of fitting a small fin under his surfboard to prevent the tail side-slipping when turning. He noticed that racing motor boats could make tight turns at high speeds because of their long skegs and he adapted this idea for his surfboard. Since then the shape and position of the skeg, and the material of which it is made, have become an inexhaustible subject of discussion among crack surfers. Boardsailing would be impossible without a skeg because the board would not stay on course at speed but would continually yaw back and forth, or sheer off to one side. On the other hand a skeg should be no larger than necessary because it has to offer as little resistance to the water as possible. It is the distance between the daggerboard and the skeg that determines how well a board will turn; the closer the skeg to the daggerboard the greater the manoeuvrability but the less will be the directional stability.

Unlike the loose daggerboard most sailboards have a fixed skeg which cannot be adjusted, or at most very slightly; nor is there any choice as to shape. Some boards have a skeg which lifts, rather like a pivoting centreboard, when it strikes an object. This is very useful when surfsailing, for example, when starting from the beach or running right up onto the shore. A lifting skeg is pointless, however, if you have to reach under the board to raise it. Some skegs can be lifted out from above but most cannot be adjusted at all. The only other point to remember is that pointed skegs with sharp edges can cause injuries.

The daggerboard

This is a small plastic or wooden board which is pushed down into the water through a slot in the centre of the board called the daggerboard trunk or case. Daggerboards protrude about 50 cm (20 ins) beneath the board and provide lateral resistance to discourage the board from being blown sideways, especially when sailing close-hauled; that is they reduce leeway. A good daggerboard is streamlined, faired and smoothed symmetrically. Like sails they are made in a variety of shapes and sizes. The normal daggerboard is used when racing; a smaller, shorter shape is used for surfsailing, partly because of the danger of running onto the beach and partly because the greater resistance of the larger normal-sized daggerboard would only reduce the very high speeds attained by sailsurfing experts. Latterly a combination type daggerboard or centreboard has appeared. You step on one or other side of a pivot to raise or lower the centreboard as desired. Thus you can sail out to sea against the wind with a draft of 60 cm (24 ins) but, just by stepping on it, you can raise it to sailsurf back to the shore again at high speed drawing only 20 cm (8 ins).

The great advantage of the centreboard which pivots is that, if it is left down unintentionally when you charge into the shore or run onto a sandbank it will automatically lift up and aft. With a fixed daggerboard you would certainly damage the daggerboard trunk severely.

Wooden daggerboards should be properly varnished, especially after they have been damaged, to prevent water penetrating and softening the wood. Only top quality wood or marine plywood should be used. Plastic daggerboards should only be used if they are hollow or foam-filled becase they must always float.

Daggerboards vary greatly in size and shape, both according to the manufacturer and to the purpose for which they are designed. *Left,* a small storm daggerboard. *Centre,* two normal daggerboards produced by different manufacturers. *Right,* a pivoting centreboard.

Rigging the sailboard

- Take with you:
  Two spare one metre lengths of 6 mm diameter rope.
  Matches.
  Adhesive tape.

Once you know how to rig a sailboard it only takes minutes to do. The assembly instructions provided by most sailboard manufacturers should not be thrown away because, later on, you will at least know the name of the manufacturer should your local sailboard supplier have difficulty in obtaining spare parts.

To prevent the ends of synthetic rope from unlaying, melt and fuse the yarns together over a naked flame or with hot cutters. For boardsailing all you require is braided rope of two sizes, 6 mm and 10 mm in diameter ($\frac{3}{4}$ inch and $1\frac{1}{4}$ inch in circumference). The complete set that you will need consists of:

Uphaul—$1\frac{1}{4}''$–$1\frac{1}{2}''$ circ. (10–12 mm dia), $4'$–$4'6''$ long before being knotted.

Uphaul shock cord—$\frac{1}{2}''$–$\frac{3}{4}''$ circ. (4–6 mm dia), about $20''$ long.

Inhaul, downhaul, outhaul, and the safety line to connect the rig to the board—$\frac{3}{4}''$ circ. (6 mm dia), all $20''$ to $30''$ long.

Knots

It is absolutely essential to know which special knots to use and to learn how to tie them. Seamen's knots have been tested and proved over the centuries and they differ from other knots in that they can generally be untied, even when wet, once the tension on the rope has been eased. You will need the following:

Rolling hitch
Bowline
Figure of eight
Half hitch

See the photos at right.

Practise assembling the rig in the garden or on the beach. Look at the instructions.

If masts are made in sections these have to be assembled first. Some masts have a separate mast foot and mast tip which have to be fitted. It is advisable to seal all joints with waterproof tape, not just to protect the sail from sharp edges but to prevent water entering the mast. The rig must not sink!

Now attach the inhaul to the mast using a rolling hitch, or a clove hitch with a stopper knot. The position is usually marked on the mast but, if not, lay the mast along the sleeve in the sail with the mast tip exactly at the top of the sail. The inhaul is made fast at the cut-out in the sleeve, and the boom will later be attached there as well. Then feed the mast into the sleeve and, using a bowline, attach

A clove hitch with a stopper knot (figure of eight) in the end is an alternative to the rolling hitch which is used to attach the inhaul to the mast.

Bowline—a non-slip loop in a line. This knot is used to attach the downhaul and outhaul to the sail.

Figure of eight knot—prevents a line unreeving through an eye or cleat. Used on the end of the uphaul.

A half turn and two half hitches—a useful knot used for example to make the outhaul fast instead of cleating it. It is more secure if a complete turn and a half is made round the spar.

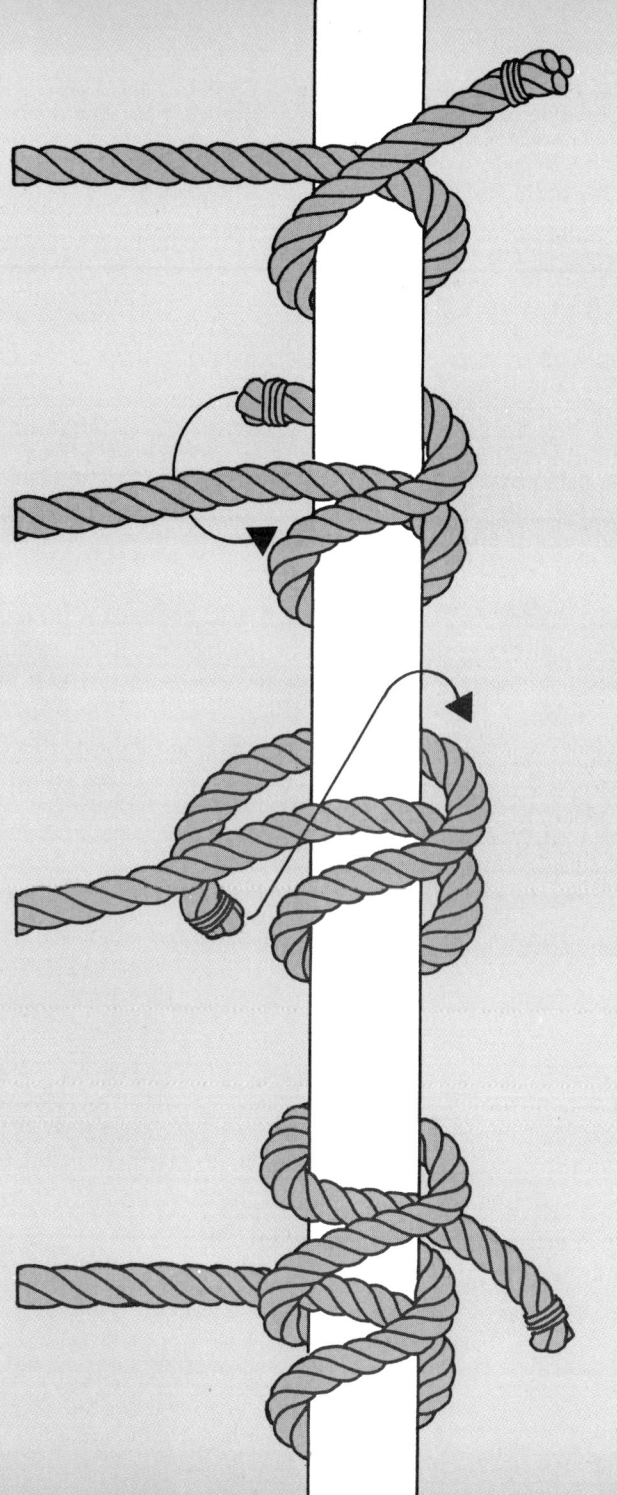

How to make a rolling hitch which can be used to fasten the inhaul to the mast.

one of the thin 6 mm ($\frac{3}{4}$ inch dia.) lines as a downhaul to the tack cringle near the bottom of the mast sleeve. The other end of the downhaul is made fast with two half hitches to the eye lower down the mast and above the mast foot. It is best to lead the line back and forth at least twice through the tack cringle and the eye so that it acts as a sort of multiple tackle without sheaves. You can then more easily and accurately adjust the tension of the luff to match the wind strength.

Place the wishbone boom around mast and sail before tying the most important knot of all which holds the boom to the mast. The boom must not be able to work free from the mast while you are out sailing, and the knot must not give—not even a fraction. The boom has to fit as snugly to the mast as possible, so first pull the rolling hitch on the mast as tight as you can to prevent it slipping and then lead the end of the inhaul through the eye on the boom, pull it really taut, and cleat it firmly in the jam cleat on the boom. This will be still firmer if you pass the line once or twice round the mast and through the eye or end fitting on the boom before cleating it.

Next attach the uphaul and the sail outhaul. The uphaul is led from below, up through the space in the forward part of the boom, and a figure of eight knot is tied in the end to prevent it coming out. The uphaul is used to raise the rig from the water and to hold it before you

Top: The boom should fit as snugly to the mast as possible. The rolling hitch or clove hitch, must not slip so a figure of eight is tied in the end. It is best to pass the inhaul twice round the mast.

Bottom: An alternative method. The line is first fastened to the boom loop, then wrapped round the mast and the loop twice before going to the cleat.

Opposite: The uphaul is led from below through the eye in the boom end fitting, and a figure of eight knot is tied in the end to prevent it coming out. Many sails have two cut-out sections in the mast sleeve, one for tall and the other for shorter boardsailors.

get under way, and you will find it easier to haul on if you tie three or four simple overhand knots along it.

The small piece of shock cord serves as an automatic retriever for the uphaul. One end is attached to the second overhand knot in the uphaul and the other end is made fast to the eye above the mast foot. The shock cord will keep the uphaul within reach when the rig is lying in the water.

The outhaul for the sail is attached to the clew cringle with a bowline in just the same way as the downhaul. Lead it through the outer end fitting on the boom and make it fast in the jam cleat on the boom or, if there is no cleat, make a clove hitch round the lashing. Now the rig is ready.

Your first attempts on the water will be in light breezes so do not pull the downhaul and outhaul too taut. Just enough tension to enable the sail to set with the minimum of creases.

A safety line is only wanted when the water is rough, as in surf, or in strong winds when the board would be blown downwind quickly if the rig became detached from the board. Like a safety strap used when skiing it serves to prevent board and rig becoming separated, which can happen when the mast foot jumps out or is released from the step.

Above: Three or four knots spaced along the uphaul give a better grip when hauling the sail out of the water. The shock cord is fitted between the uphaul and the mast foot to keep the uphaul within reach at all times when the rig is lying in the water.

Left: The sail outhaul is attached to the clew of the sail with a bowline. Here it is led back and forth twice between the clew cringle and the outer boom end fitting and is then made fast with two half hitches round itself.

When transporting a sailboard on the roof of a car safety is only guaranteed if a special or suitable roof rack is used. This is a good way of carrying the mast.

Transport

Although boardsailing is a sport that can be enjoyed without a car, one of its attractions, and the way it has caught on, is due to the convenience of modern transport. Unlike a normal boat owner you have no problems over moorings and storage. Instead all you need is to acquire a good roof-rack.

Another of the delights of boardsailing is that it is so easy to load your sailboard onto the car, and you are then free to drive rapidly along a motorway to the sea, or make your way along narrow tracks to some lonely inland water, according to your mood of the moment. The most important point is that your roof-rack must hold the sailboard firmly to the car without damaging it because a great deal of lift is generated when driving at high speeds on fast roads. The roof-rack must not work loose on rough roads, nor should it slip forward a fraction of an inch in the rain gutters on the car roof when you brake hard. If you are to avoid scratching the board when loading and unloading it the roof-rack must have no sharp edges.

Advice: it is not worth trying to be economical! It is best to buy a roof-rack that has proved satisfactory and you could benefit from asking other experienced boardsailors for their opinions.

- Lash the board down firmly with broad strong straps that will not chafe or slip.
- Load the board upside down with the bow forwards. The mast lies beside it and the boom on top unless your roof-rack has a special boom holder.

When you reach the water and have assembled your rig remember two simple rules:

- Carry the rig and the board to the water separately. It is far too awkward carrying a sailboard with its mast stepped, even if there is only a short way to go.
- Always put the rig in the water first and the board afterwards because the mast is not stepped until both rig and board are floating in the water. Also the board has more windage than the rig and drifts downwind faster, The rig floats in the water, rather than on it like the board, and will stay where you put it, even in strong winds.

If the water is not too far away you can easily carry the rig above your head with the sail extended, holding the boom with one hand and the mast with the other. If you point the foot of the mast, or the mast itself, towards the wind, the wind will help you by supporting the sail.

If the water is some distance away leave the sail rolled round the mast and the boom folded up against it. Carry them to the water's edge like this, and you can then extend the sail fully there.

Most boards can be carried easily under one arm with your hand in the daggerboard slot. If you find this too heavy or too awkward, slip the daggerboard into the slot and this will

18

Top: When the rig is assembled, carry it like this, one hand on the mast, the other on the boom, holding the rig above your head with the mast foot pointing towards the wind so that it helps support the sail.

Centre: It is better to carry the rig folded up like this, if there is far to go to the water's edge.

Bottom: The sailboard only weighs 22–28 kg (48–62 lbs) and can easily be carried with one hand in the daggerboard slot.

give you a good hand hold. If you are sailing in company it is easy to carry two boards at the same time, each person taking the end of one board under one arm and the end of the second board under the other arm.

Tools and spares

Think for a moment—you have just discovered a small tear in the sail. If you go sailing it could easily rip right across. What is more the boat stores are shut and you would have to go home to get some adhesive tape because you have not even got any surgical tape in your first aid kit in the car. Or worse still—you are boardsailing on a superb day and the outhaul breaks—chafed through! Have you spoilt your weekend?

A practical boardsailor would undoubtedly have a spare line tucked into his wet suit or attached to the boom as well as some tools and spares on the beach ready for making repairs. You only need to be able to

put minor damage right. Dealing with major damage to the board such as replacing a broken or lost universal joint, daggerboard, or even the mast itself, inevitably means a more serious delay. In making a list for a mini-breakdown kit we should differentiate between what is essential and what is desirable:

- Essential
  Spare 6 mm (¾ inch circ.) rope for downhaul or inhaul.
  Matches for fusing rope ends.
  Knife and small screwdriver.
  Adhesive tape for temporary sail repairs.
- Desirable
  Anti-slip wax for the board.
  Spare battens (if fitted).
  Taping to make handholds on the boom.
  Pieces of sail cloth, with waterproof adhesive, to repair the sail.
  Filler to stop up holes in the board.

Clothing

Are you thick-skinned? Are you tough? Do you weigh a good 80 kg (13 stone) with an above average layer of fat? Perhaps you are sure that swimming pants will be O.K. for boardsailing because you swim outdoors from March to October anyway. Make no mistake—thinking this way could lead to trouble with your kidneys. Not even the thickest of skins is insulated enough for boardsailing in cooler latitudes far from the equator and a wet suit is essential in the long term, even in summer temperatures.

When boardsailing, the real purpose of clothing is to prevent loss of body heat when the boardsailor comes into contact with spray or when swimming. The temperature of the air is rarely as high as that of our bodies, 37°C, even in intense sunshine and, even on those occasions, the boardsailor would frizzle on the sunny side but be cold on the shaded side and therefore lose body heat. The cold that results from evaporation of spray is the worst enemy of boardsailors, particularly from strong wind addicts and beginners who generally do more swimming than sailing. This is why you need a second skin, although a thin one is enough in high summer.

Wet suits are usually made of foam neoprene. The insulation being provided by the air trapped in the expanded foam layer.

Garments of polyurethane coated nylon, or thin stretch-materials, are extremely pliable, smart and convenient, but are only really suitable for summer temperatures.

Single-lined neoprene is lined on the inside with nylon, but double-lined neoprene has a nylon lining on the outside as well. Water runs off a plain neoprene surface so quickly that there is no loss of body heat due to evaporation with the single-lined neoprene. But the double lined, though harder wearing, causes the body to take longer to regain its original temperature after falling in or being wet by spray. Apart from types with a shiny outer lining, off which water drips immediately, material lined on the inside only is preferable because body heat is lowered for a shorter period. Material 3–4 mm thick is quite adequate for the temperatures experienced during the normal boardsailing season.

A two-part suit is best, that is a Long John plus a bolero top. The Long John reaches to the shoulders and has full length legs, but the arms are left completely free. It is easier to put on if it has a zip fastener down the front, and this can be unzipped to provide ventilation if you get very hot. A light windcheater can be worn on top or, on colder days, a bolero top with full-length sleeves.

A wet suit should be a good fit because any water that penetrates causes body temperature to drop. Make sure that the sleeves and legs are cut sufficiently generously to give the freedom of movement needed when boardsailing. Bolero sleeves, in particular, must have zip fasteners so that they can be opened when necessary to avoid constricting the forearms. Knee and shin guards are useful, and so is a pocket for your car key.

Insulation is the most important factor. Elasticity, resistance to tearing and buoyancy are always greater than is required in practice.

Shoes

It feels fine to stand on the board and let the water swirl over your bare feet. In the summer, when the wind is light and the water warm, bare feet are always best but the harder the wind blows and the colder the water the more essential it is to wear shoes. You will enjoy boardsailing in strong winds and waves only if you have a sure foothold, and in the spring and

Above: A neoprene wet suit provides warmth and is absolutely essential when boardsailing. This Long John has a practical long zip down the front. The bolero top is only required on colder days.

Centre: Excellent warm gloves with leather palms and neoprene backs for cold days. Gloves are unnecessary in normal summer temperatures.

Right: Special boardsailing shoes made of nylon and soft chamois leather. The rubber soles have small suckers to discourage slipping.

autumn your feet simply get too cold if you wear no shoes. Decide whether you want non-slip, warmth, or both when you buy shoes.

It is much easier to stand barefoot on polyethylene than on GRP, but it is still possible to aquaplane on the board on occasions. Special shoes not

only slip less but help to prevent injury, for example when you knock against the mast foot. Training shoes with flexible shoes are perfectly adequate. Special boardsailing shoes must fit well and should grip well, but be sure that they are really flexible. Shoes with neoprene uppers keep the feet warm, but water almost always collects in them and this naturally affects your grip. In all cases, wax may be needed in addition.

Simple neoprene socks are not suitable for boardsailing because your toes work forward and soon force holes in them. They are only suitable for use as socks inside a pair of shoes, and the Long John should then be pulled down over them.

Gloves

Gloves are a problem for boardsailors because anything between the boom and your hands interferes with your grip when sailing and your hold is then less secure. You can sometimes get blisters more quickly if you wear gloves than when you do not. It is best to take care of your hands and wait patiently until they have hardened thoroughly. Use a good cream regularly.

If you must wear gloves the cheapest are the most effective. Ordinary household rubber gloves can be obtained anywhere and they give you an excellent grip on the boom, even on bare aluminium, as well as clinging well to the fingers and being completely wind and waterproof.

Winter gloves are generally made of neoprene and are really only needed on exceptionally cold days.

Boardsailing for beginners

Your newly-purchased board and rig are lying in the water, the sun is shining and there is a wonderful sailing breeze. You are standing on the board in your swimming gear, having already fallen in ten times and are trying to raise the sail for the eleventh time. Phew, it is hard work! Gradually you pull the rig out of the water but, suddenly, you lose your balance and—splash, yet another swim! Just then an experienced boardsailor whisks past on his board, hanging lazily from the boom and leaning out slightly over the water, relaxed and effortlessly graceful while you, though seething with envy, are fascinated.

Leaning out on the boom over the water the experienced boardsailor planes gracefully and effortlessly over the lake—much to the envy of the beginner. But boardsailing is easy to learn, and even experts had to suffer many a ducking when they started.

But this is how everyone starts, and that includes not only your experienced boardsailor but present and future champions. They will fall, take many an unintentional bath and practise landing in the water, but this is absolutely normal and just part of learning. Always remember that to begin with boardsailing is synonymous with falling in because you have to learn first how to balance. This is equally true for those who have sailed in ordinary boats. Their knowledge and sailing experience give them no advantage to begin with.

Depending on your teacher and your speed of learning this phase may last anything from ten minutes to three hours. You can of course learn by trial and error, taking no advice. You will certainly learn how to sail your board, but will probably develop technical faults which soon become deeply engrained and which, when sailing in strong winds later on, prevent you from making further progress. If you have instruction you will learn to boardsail more quickly and will not spend hours or even days struggling over the same problem.

A course of instruction is built up in progressive stages and, as each is based on what has already been learnt, the order cannot be altered. For example it is pointless to try to sail a straight course as soon as you have hoisted the sail out of the water because you must first be able to turn the board round in the water. Once you can turn the board on the spot you can change your course as you wish without using your sails, whatever the situation in which you find yourself.

You will find that you become much less frustrated if you learn in company, and group instruction has other advantages as well. Not only is it more fun to see other people falling in too, which makes you less annoyed with yourself, but you will recognise your own mistakes when others make them, and so learn as you watch.

The most important point about having instruction is that you learn in safety. Part of the rig may break, you may drift away from land in an offshore wind—and that can happen much more quickly than you would believe possible, or the abnormal exertion may exhaust you so much that you cannot swim and pull your board back to the shore. If other competent boardsailors have you under constant observation they can come to your rescue.

Where to learn

The ideal area for beginners is a bay with wide sandy beaches sloping into the water, no groynes and few swimmers. Unsuitable areas which should be avoided are those where there are large stones or rocks above or below water, waters where there are currents, tidal streams or nearby shipping, and above all any type of shore such as a quay wall made of stones or rocks. A sandy beach is perfect because there is a soft landing everywhere and the hull will not be damaged. The fewer the swimmers the smaller the danger of running into them before gaining full control of the sailboard.

Try also to find somewhere where the water is the right depth. You need

hip-deep or chest-deep water over a gently shelving sea-bed so that you do not get out of your depth until you are well offshore. Shallow water allows you to get back onto your board easily after the inevitable falls, and saves energy. With a beach of this sort you can also let yourself be blown to leeward some way when practising without getting out of your depth, and so save yourself the bother of continually having to pull your board back into shallower water to start again.

The wind and sailing area

A light breeze is best to begin with (see the wind force scale given in the appendix). A flat calm is unsuitable because you need some pressure on the sail to get moving. On the other hand a wind of nearly force 4 is too strong. The direction of the wind is also important. A sailor differentiates between an offshore, or land, breeze and an onshore, or sea, breeze. A land breeze blows directly, or at an angle, from the land to the water and its full force is only felt some distance from the land, particularly if the coast is steep and high. Close under the shore will be beautifully smooth, even in a strong wind, because wind has to blow some distance over water before waves build up.

Perfect for beginners! A light breeze and smooth warm water—you can even enjoy falling in.

One cannot overemphasize the danger of being blown offshore. At first the beginner is much more concerned with raising his sail from the water and balancing it upright than with sailing forwards and, in consequence, he is driven to leeward. If the wind is blowing from the land he will always be blown further away from the shore and there is therefore always a danger of not being able to get back.

Onshore winds blow at an angle to or directly onto the shore. And so a tired beginner will be blown back towards the safety of land. So an onshore breeze is never dangerous. It is a reliable rescue service provided by nature. Unfortunately onshore winds also mean rough water, which makes it more difficult for the beginner to get his balance. On smaller inland waters no appreciable waves will form to disturb a learner when the wind is light, but on larger lakes, and in the open sea especially, even force 2 or 3 winds make the water choppy, and it is then almost impossible for a beginner to stand upright. On the other hand the wind will be steadier because it blows over open water and is not disturbed by obstructions.

A *land*, or *offshore* breeze is quite different and is often extremely gusty which is irritating. Houses and trees on the bank, or differences in the height of the land, in fact every irregularity in the silhouette of the shore will deflect and disturb the wind so that it blows in fits and starts. In spite of the calmer water the beginner finds this difficult because it is harder to learn in fitful, puffy conditions. By beginner we mean anyone who cannot make his own way back under sail to his starting point on the shore. Generally speaking an offshore wind is only suitable for beginners when it is under about force 3 because he would then be able to paddle or swim, pushing his board back to the shore. The ideal wind is one that blows parallel to the shore.

■ To sum up, there are three requirements for perfect sailing conditions in which beginners can learn most easily: a sandy beach, light winds preferably parallel to the shore and reasonably calm water.

If you are going boardsailing on a large lake or at the coast do not just find out about the prevailing wind

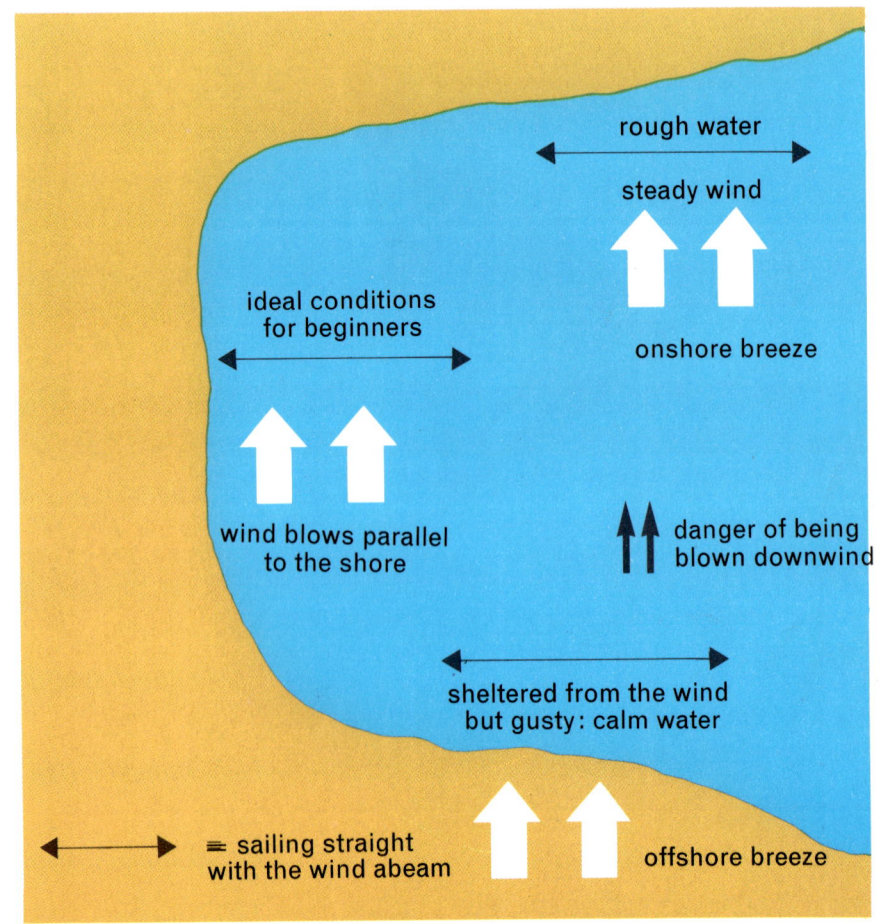

A combination of light breezes and calm water provides ideal conditions for learning. Best is when the wind is blowing parallel to the shore. An offshore wind is dangerous.

but study the map too and look for a suitable part of the shore. As you will probably be motoring anyway it is well worth while driving to a place where the wind is right and the water quiet.

Balancing with the rig

Enough of forethought and preparation—it is time to take to the water! First you must learn how to balance, because boardsailing is first and foremost a balancing act. Strength plays a far less important part than the art and technique of balancing. At first it seems absolutely contradictory that when boardsailing not only do you support the rig but you use the rig to support yourself. This balancing act is a feature only of boardsailing; sailing a normal boat is not the same. The two things you have to co-ordinate are, first, to stand steadily and move about on the wobbly board and, secondly, to support and handle the rig.

These two skills should be practised separately because you then do not have to cope with the difficulties of balancing the board and supporting the rig simultaneously. It does not matter which you try first, so let us start with the rig on dry land.

You do not need the board, only the rig itself set on the mast and boom. First learn how to hold and handle the rig correctly which includes raising the rig with the uphaul, grasping the boom correctly and simulating getting under way. Practising on dry land makes good sense because you do not fall into the water as soon as you make a mistake.

Of all the various steps in learning this is the only one that a beginner can try in stronger winds. Lay the rig on the ground in such a way that the mast foot points towards the direction from which the wind is blowing, that is pointing to windward, while the mast top points in the direction to which it is blowing, to leeward. Make a small hole in the ground for the mast foot to act as a substitute for the mast step in the board. Then the rig will not slip away so easily when you are pulling it up.

Now stand with your back to the wind, facing the rig to leeward, with the mast foot between your feet. This is just the same position as you will be in later when on the water, except that your rig will be stepped into the slot in the board and the board will be lying across the wind.

Take hold of the *uphaul* with both hands and pull, raising the rig until the boom is clear of the ground, the mast being almost upright and the sail shaking freely in the wind. If the mast foot starts slipping towards you while you are pulling up the rig brace your foot against it. Hold the mast close to you with your elbows slightly bent. Gently swing it to right and left, but make sure that the boom does not touch the ground or catch on anything.

To simulate getting under way you will need to have both hands on the boom holding the sail against the pressure of the wind. In order to do this let go of the uphaul with one hand, (for this exercise it does not matter which) so that you are balancing the rig by the uphaul with only one hand. Your free hand then crosses over the hand holding the uphaul and catches hold of the boom close to the mast, about 10–15 cm (4–6 ins) behind it.

This hand is called the *mast hand*. Let us say that you let go with your right hand and are supporting the rig by the uphaul only with your left. Your right hand will then become the mast hand. Your left hand can now release the uphaul and you support the rig by holding the boom with your mast hand, your right hand, only (see the photos following).

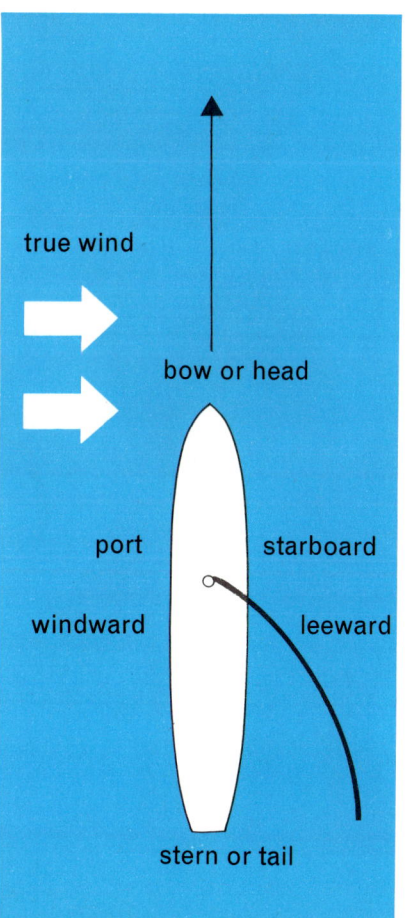

Practising on land

This is how to simulate getting under way.

1. Hold the rig close to your body (right) by gripping the uphaul with both hands and keep your elbows bent. The sail flaps.

4. Then release the uphaul with your left hand and balance the rig with your right hand only.

5. Now the most important point: pull the mast past your shoulder and to windward. The sail is still fluttering freely.

2. Release the uphaul with one hand, in this case your right (the mast hand).

3. Catch hold of the boom 10–15 cm (4–6 ins) behind the mast.

6. Only now do you catch hold of the boom with your left hand, (the sheet hand).

7. Sheet in the sail until it is just beginning to fill with wind.

This is how the sail is balanced against the wind when practising on the beach. Keeping it balanced in stronger breezes is great fun and, when the technique is learnt, can be done easily by beginners.

You must still keep the rig clear of the ground and allow the sail to shake freely in the wind, just as you did when you were balancing the rig with the uphaul. Your left hand is then free to grasp the boom further away from the mast and can pull in the sail. When doing this job it is called the sail or *sheet hand*.

Later, when boardsailing, your right and left hands exchange jobs as mast and sheet hands every time you turn the board and stand on the opposite side, that is, every time you tack and gybe.

Even when practising on land just holding the rig and balancing it against the wind pressure is quite tricky. When viewed from what would be ahead of the board the mast should be absolutely upright and tilted forward (towards what would be the bow) far enough for the boom to be about parallel to the ground. When the wind blows harder the boom pulls strongly against your hands and arms but balancing the rig is practically entirely a matter of correct technique; strength is less important.

The first typical beginner's mistake is to give way with your mast hand when the pressure of the wind on the sail becomes excessive. This is quite wrong because the rig then just pivots to about your sheet hand, the mast goes to leeward, the sail swings across the wind, and will immediately pull you over the 'board' on top of the falling sail. So when the wind pressure becomes too great and you feel that you cannot hold on much longer, continue to hold on firmly with your mast hand, but ease out your sheet arm. Boardsailors call this *sheeting out* or *easing out* the sail. The wind will then no longer fill all the area of the sail, the pressure on the rig is reduced and you will be able to hold it more easily. It is the sheet hand alone that eases out the sail, pivoting around the mast hand, and it should be done slowly and smoothly, not jerkily, or you will finish up on the ground—and later in the water.

In stronger winds of force 3–4 and more it is not enough to fill the sail just by raking the mast forward with your mast hand and sheeting in as described. The correct technique is to pull the boom and rig to windward past your shoulder with your mast hand. Then when you sheet in the sail by pulling in the boom with your sheet hand you have to brace your front leg firmly against the mast foot and lean back well to windward to balance the greater wind pressure.

Mast to windward is the secret of boardsailing technique in stronger winds.

As a beginner you will find practising on land easier if you have a friend helping to hold the mast foot firm. You can also step the mast in the board instead of sticking it into the ground. Place the board at right angles to the wind, step the mast, stand on the board (after cleaning your shoes) and off you go as already described.

■ Note: It is absolutely essential to check that you start in the correct position with the board at right angles to the wind, your back to the wind and the rig to leeward (the *mast abeam* position).

Sailboard schools often use a simulator which is either a complete sailboard or the standing area of a board, set up so that it can turn and tilt in all directions, but limited by springs or small hydraulic dampers. The learner standing slightly raised above the ground, can then try to steer the sailboard by raking the rig.

The second typical beginner's mistake is to stand with backside stuck

Unsteady boardsailors are easily pulled by the boom into this ungainly position (right) by the lightest of gusts—bottom out, arms straight and trunk bent forward towards the sail.

These five boardsailors are sailing close hauled and they have adopted very different stances. Sailing with their hips straight or bent all of them are leaning back towards the wind. This is the only way that it is possible to counter the pull on the wishbone boom when the wind blows harder.

out, legs straight, and the trunk bent well forward by the tug of the boom on the arms.

This is quite wrong and if you stand like this any small gust or slight increase in the wind will whip you off the board. When your body is so bent you cannot begin to exert the force needed to counter the boom's strong pull. Boardsailors only bend their hips if, at the same time, they bend their knees and lean backwards—as you will be able to see in the photographs. Use the correct technique from the start. Keep your hips straight, lean your body backwards and keep your arms slightly bent. Do not hang at full stretch on the boom like a wet sack.

If your technique is right from the start you will find it much easier later on to overcome the force 4 hurdle when learning strong wind techniques and will enjoy all the sooner the fun of planing on your sailboard at high speed. Dry land practice enables you to get this technique right and even to simulate getting under way and sailing the board in a straight line.

Trying to balance on the board for the first time is not easy, even when kneeling, but it is important to practise this. The board is more wobbly like this than with the rig in place.

Balancing on the board

The board alone on the water is all you need for this exercise. The object is to get the feel of the board's motion when it is afloat, to learn how to mount it correctly and to learn to stand on it relatively steadily.

 Find a spot where the water is knee-deep or hip-deep. Always mount the board from the side, near the daggerboard slot and rest in a sitting position on the board with both feet in the water; just pulling your legs onto the board makes it slightly more wobbly. Now kneel with the daggerboard slot between your legs and hold the board rails (the side edges) with both hands, tilting the board deliberately to right and left so that you can feel how it reacts.

 Then stand up. To start with, balance with your arms outstretched. Now try whatever movements you like to get used to the board's re-actions; for example :-
—turn yourself right round
—move as far as possible towards the bow

It is easier to balance on the board if you keep your arms stretched out like this. Beginners start falling in when they try this because there is nothing to hold on to.

—move as far as possible towards the stern
—jump up and down
—jump and turn, first through 90° and then a complete half turn
—try a headstand

The daggerboard helps to damp down the wobbling. So when it is out the board is less stable. Later on, when you have fitted the dagger and stepped the rig in the board and it is lying in the water, you will find that you have even more stability, but a boardsailor can never be too steady on his feet so it is worth practising on a bare board.

Another point: when there is no wind at all your board makes a good swimming float for the children. But never use the board like this when an offshore breeze is blowing. If you take out the daggerboard, and perhaps unscrew the skeg, there will be no chance of injury when the board turns upside down and the children can play on it without worry.

Paddling

Paddling is also part of learning how to handle your board. Every boardsailor must be able to paddle his sailboard, at least for a short distance, and also against fresher winds. There is no alternative if you are unable to sail when, for example, the wind drops or you have a broken mast foot. If you underestimate the strength of the wind, or it shifts to blow from the land and freshens, you could find yourself exhausted and have no grip left in your hands for holding the rig.

You can paddle almost anywhere with one exception; you cannot reach a distant shore when there is a strong offshore wind. Even if you make yourself as small as possible and stow the rig completely, the windage of the floating board alone is enough to drive it downwind. In all other cases your hands can serve effectively as paddles, but the rig must first be stowed tidily. So, to paddle:

- If the wind is light or you have not got too far to go:
  Unstep the rig and free the outhaul from the end of the boom, roll the sail round the mast and lash it firmly. Ease the inhaul slightly and fold the boom up to the mast where you tie it securely. Lay the rig lengthwise on the board, mast foot forward, kneel across it and paddle. If the distance is short it does not matter whether you leave the daggerboard in the slot or not.

- If the wind is stronger or there is further to go:
  Use the mast as a paddle. The rig therefore has to be taken completely to pieces. Fold the sail up as small as possible and put it on the board with the boom and daggerboard. You can sit or kneel on them while you paddle with the mast. This is not a perfect solution because the whole load can slip off

Paddle like this if there is not too far to go. First pack up the rig: free the outhaul, roll the sail round the mast, fold the boom up to it and, when they are lashed together, lay them lengthwise on the board. Paddle with your hands.

easily in a strong wind and waves. Unrigging also takes precious time during which the board will drift quite some distance further downwind.

The safest method in a strong offshore wind is to lie flat on the board and paddle, not frantically but strongly and above all continuously, to keep the board moving through the water. Regardless of where you are aiming, point the head of the board dead into the wind and waves because only in this way can you keep your windage to the minimum and have some chance of making headway. Paddle like this until you are close under the shore, even if you originally started from some quite different place. The wind and waves will decrease close to the land and you can then paddle back parallel to the shore to your departure point without risking being blown offshore again.

Towing

A few sailboards have a towing eye fitted to the bow. They can be towed easily by hand or on the end of a towrope attached to a boat. They can be towed at speed but the whole rig and the daggerboard should be taken aboard the towing boat. Fast motor boats should use a very short towrope so that only the stern of the board lies on the water.

Obviously towing is impossible if the board has no towing eye. Never attempt to hold the board by hand or to tow it with a rope through the daggerboard slot. It is better to load board and all into the rescuing boat. If the boat towing is a slow dinghy or another sailboard (not a fast planing dinghy) the rig is prepared as for paddling, the boardsailor lies down full length on it and he then holds on to a tow rope from the dinghy, or made fast to the daggerboard strap on a rescuing sailboard.

Raising the sail

Now put the board with the rig stepped and the daggerboard pushed down into the trunk, afloat into hip-deep water.

The object is to raise the rig out of the water with the minimum of effort and support the mast so that the sail is shaking in the wind. Then your sailboard will be absolutely ready to get under way. But, think first please, and then everything will go much more smoothly.

You will have carried the extended rig to the water above your head at arms length, with one hand on the boom and the other on the mast. The mast joint or the mast itself must point towards the wind when you do this, while the end of the boom points to leeward.

The start position is with the rig to leeward of the board with the mast foot pointing towards the board, so place the rig in the water to leeward

Before starting to haul the rig out of the water make sure that the mast foot is between your feet because only then will the pull be directly over the mast joint. If the pull is forward or aft of the mast foot the rig will be dragged round towards the board.

of the board. Then turn the board so that it is at right angles to the wind direction, and you will find it very easy to fit the mast foot into the step. Get onto the board from windward, stand up with your back to the wind with the mast joint between your feet, take hold of the uphaul and you are in the right position for raising the sail. You will notice how much more stable the board is now that the rig is lying in the water beside it, and this makes the job of raising the sail while balancing on the board very much easier.

Crouch low and keep your arms straight to start with. Then gradually straighten your legs as you pull until the entire rig is clear of the water.

There are two important points to remember:

- Haul slowly at first, but steadily so that the water can drain off the sail and out of the sleeve. After this you will find that the sail can be pulled up much more easily and may well jerk suddenly right out of the water. You must be prepared for this and ease the pull because otherwise you will immediately fly backwards into the water with the sail on top of you.
- While raising the sail by hauling on the uphaul the mast must stay virtually at right angles to the board because, otherwise, the board would start to turn away

from its position across the wind. In others words, the direction of pull must always be exactly over the universal joint and not to right or left of it. Otherwise the board could pivot round beneath the sail to a position from which it could be difficult or impossible to start sailing. Should the rig slip to one side in the water while you are raising it, deliberately pull it the opposite way to get the board back to the correct cross-wind position again.

Finally you should be standing upright on the board, still with the mast joint between your feet, holding the rig with both hands high on the

1. Raise the sail. The boardsailor is standing in the correct position with the board lying across the wind and the sail in the water at right angles to the board.

2. Crouch at first and pull slowly but steadily, keeping your arms straight, and let the water drain off the sail.

A typical beginner's fall. After the water has drained off the sail the rig suddenly becomes much lighter. This beginner has continued to pull hard and as a result falls backwards into the water and the sail will come on top of him.

3. Suddenly the sail becomes much lighter and the boardsailor has to pull more carefully. The water now drains out of the sleeve.

4. The sail is pulled up directly over the mast joint so that the board stays at right angles to the wind. Only the tip of the boom is trailing in the water.

5. The sail is absolutely clear of the water and fluttering in the wind at right angles to the board as he holds it with both hands at the top of the uphaul.

uphaul. You can allow the mast to lean slightly (as seen from ahead) but the boom must not touch the water. The sail will then be free to flutter in the wind at right angles to the board. It is largely a matter of balance because you have to hold the shaking sail clear of the water while standing on the wobbly board. All that you need is practice.

It is best to learn with someone else or in a group, but do it the right way. It is more fun if you are not the only one to fall in and you can help each other during the early stages. On land, for example, it is much easier if a friend holds the mast while you balance the sail.

When raising the sail a helper can steady the board at the bow, but he must restrain it loosely, letting the board turn and heel quite naturally so as not to upset your balance. The important point is that he can prevent the board drifting downwind or help you to swim back with a board that has been blown away.

Mast abeam. This is the basic position which the boardsailor takes up every time before getting under way.

Lifting the sail to windward

It is when raising the rig from the water that beginners go for a swim most often. The jerk when the sail comes clear of the water keeps on catching them unawares and they fall backwards because the resistance eases suddenly. These spills are quite normal—everybody has the same trouble to start with. In time you learn to absorb this jerk without paying for it with a swim.

If this does happen it leaves you with a different problem because your rig is then to windward, the board to leeward and you are facing the wind—exactly opposite to how you should be standing. This will cause problems when the sail fills with wind as it is lifted! There are two answers.

The easiest method is to stand on the board, facing the wind and looking at the sail to windward, with the universal joint between your feet. Raise the sail a little way out of the water by pulling on the uphaul. The wind will catch the top of the sail and push it to one side. Push with your legs to keep the mast permanently at right angles to the board and the wind will then gradually drive sail and board round together until you are back in the correct position with the rig to leeward, the board to windward and your back to the wind. Only then do you pull the sail right out of the water as usual.

The important point is to pull the sail tip no more than about half way up at first—much less when the wind is stronger—and to hold it like this while the wind turns the sailboard through 180°. This takes quite a lot of strength, and considerably more than when you simply raise the sail to leeward. There is a more elegant and expert method. First raise the sail to windward about half way, just as described, but this time you use your feet to *prevent* the board turning. Raise the sail further until only a small corner and the end of the boom are still in the water. The wind catches the sail and pushes it towards you and the board. If you now jerk the rig right out of the water it will whip across the board to leeward. At that moment you must turn like lightning ready to support the rig to leeward to prevent it from falling back into the water when it swings over. If it does fall the sail is nevertheless back on the correct side without spending time slowly turning the board round. The sail lying to leeward can then be raised in the normal way.

Unlike the first method the board does not turn round so, as well as saving time, the board will still be pointing in the original direction. A quick and neat method, but very good balance is essential.

Turning

A basic boardsailing manoeuvre is to turn the board round beneath the rig while the sail shakes freely in the wind. When the board describes a full circle this is called a 360, or 360 degree turn. You can turn your board round in all conditions even in a strong wind or a big sea.

■ First a warning; as a beginner you must never try to get under way or to sail a straight course, however much you may be tempted to do so, until you have learnt to turn your board to any direction you wish in easy conditions. The reason: until you have learnt to tack or gybe, this is the only way you will be able to turn to enable you to sail back to your departure point.

You have already discovered unintentionally how to turn the board when you started trying to raise the sail from the water. When the uphaul is not immediately above the mast joint the board reacts by turning as you pull up the sail. Also when you have raised the sail and it is fluttering freely to leeward, the board starts to turn immediately if the rig is not balanced exactly above the mast foot. This is the effect that you now use deliberately to start turning.

First stand in the mast abeam position on the board, supporting the rig with the uphaul line and letting the sail shake at right angles to the board which is lying across the wind. Let us say that the stern is to your right and the bow to your left (page 40, No 1). If you now lean the rig towards the stern the boat will start to turn slightly counter clockwise with the stern swinging away to leeward. If you rake the rig towards the bow the board will turn clockwise, the bow swinging to leeward. Make sure that the sail is absolutely free to shake and that the boom does not trail in the water.

Try this several times and you will find that the board reacts positively, Incline the mast forward and the bow

Turning the board

1 to 3, right and 4 to 7, lower row: Turning the board. It is only the board that turns: the sail merely flutters freely in the wind supported by the boardsailor who holds the uphaul close by the boom. She keeps her back to the wind all the time and faces the sail. The board is made to turn by slightly tilting the mast to one side, and she takes small steps as she moves round the mast while the board is turning. This series of photographs is a not quite perfect demonstration because the board should turn on the spot. It only sails round in a circle, as seen here, when the wind is blowing hard. (*continued*, 8 to 11 on page 42).

1.

4 to 7.

2. 3.

41

8. 9.

She continues to turn by stepping round to keep her back to the wind, and by keeping the rig raked and fluttering, the board will continue turning.

will turn to leeward, rake it aft and the bow turns to windward.

The rest is easy enough. Rake the mast aft with the sail shaking freely and the board will react by turning. Do not stand still but shuffle round so that your back is still towards the wind. Keep the mast inclined so that the board continues to turn, and go on shuffling round the mast until the board has turned as far as you wish. The sail must continue to flutter freely all the while.

During the turn the position of the sail stays virtually the same; it blows out to leeward. Your position in relation to the wind and the sail does not change either; your back is turned to the wind. The board alone will turn beneath the shaking sail while you keep the mast slightly raked and 'walk' round the board.

Be careful, though, never to let the boom end trail in the water, for more than a second or two. If this happens, or if the sail dips half way in and stays there, it is unable to shake freely, the wind will fill it and the thrust that results is converted into forward motion. Your sailboard will move forward! So, keep the end of the boom right out of the water.

Continue to practice turning in rougher water and rather stronger winds which will improve your balance enormously and you will find you can keep much better control. But always have a helper at hand; it is surprising how quickly a force 3 wind can blow a floating sailboard downwind. Beware of blowing away from the shore (you cannot yet sail back to it) or along the shore into a group of swimmers, or towards a shelving beach on which you bump your daggerboard. In stronger winds all sailboards will make headway even in the correct mast abeam position with the sail shaking, and they therefore do not turn on the spot but sail round a rather larger circle. The helper then should stay really close by the board, not holding it all the time but ready to pull it back into shallow water before it gets out of his depth. It is often better to pull a board back a short way than to have to swim or paddle a long way back to land.

Getting under way

Many beginners take far too long to become proficient because, having bought a sailboard, they start at an unsuitable area and in the wrong way. The moment of truth comes as soon as the wind starts to blow just a little harder—they cannot get going. You will have a great advantage over such beginners by having practised first on dry land, then learnt how to balance on the board and how to turn. It is all a question of technique rather than of strength, and technique can be taught. Learning is much easier if you use your brains!

This is particularly true of getting under way, and you will find just the same later when starting in strong winds because technique enables you to jump the force 4 hurdle and fully appreciate the thrills of boardsailing for the first time.

You may have already practised starting or getting under way on dry land, perhaps even on a simulator, so the procedure will not be completely strange. It is harder to start on the water in some ways because you are standing on a wobbly board and because it reacts immediately by turning every time you alter the mast rake. But given the same wind strength you do not need to use as much body weight as on dry land. Furthermore when you start successfully on the water you are immediately spurred on to keep trying, and the first time that you sail even a short stretch in a straight line you forget all the difficulties of the past and can face the prospect of future falls. If it has not already done so this is the moment when the boardsailing bug really takes hold, and you are not likely to recover from it!

■ But first hammer into your subconscious the rule about the duties of your mast hand and sheet hand. The mast hand holds firm and is the pivot, the sheet hand eases out the sail.

So you are now in the *mast abeam* position; the board across the wind, your back to the wind with the mast foot between your feet. You have raised the sail from the water and are holding the rig with both hands high on the uphaul, the flapping sail is completely clear of the water and blowing out at right angles to the board.

1. Getting moving. Begin in the *mast abeam* position.

2. The hand nearer the bow, the right hand here, will be the mast hand and grasps the boom.

3. The left hand will be the sheet hand. The rig is supported by the mast hand alone.

The method is just the same as on dry land. If the bow of the board is to your right your right hand will become the mast hand.

- *The mast hand balances the rig.* First your right hand lets go of the uphaul and you balance the rig with your left. Pass your right hand over your left and grasp the boom about 10–15 cm (4–6 ins) back from the mast. Your left hand drops the uphaul so that the rig is balanced only by your mast hand, your right hand. Keep the same basic mast abeam position with the board crosswind, your back to the wind and the sail fluttering free of the water at 90° to the board.
- *Mast to windward.* Now comes the most important moment. Your mast hand pulls the rig to windward past your shoulders until the boom is parallel to the water. With your arm bent your mast hand will be quite close to your shoulder, while the sail will still be shaking. When you do this your body will turn slightly towards the direction in which you will sail.
- *Sheet hand graps the boom.* Now catch hold of the boom with your left or sheet hand, about three feet further aft than the mast hand.
- *Sheet hand pulls in the sail.* Pull in the boom slightly with your sheet hand. The sail then fills with wind and the board will start to move. It will travel straight ahead provided the boom is parallel to the water and the mast therefore is raked slightly forward. Do not pull the boom in suddenly (sheeting in) but slowly and gradually so that you get the feel of the wind pressure and can adjust your balance more easily.

At the actual moment of starting

4. Now, most important: the mast is pulled to windward past her shoulder. The sail is still shaking.

5. Only then does her sheet hand grasp the boom.

6. She sheets in the sail slowly until it is full of wind.

you have to transmit the pull of the sail from the boom, through your body and via your forward leg to the board, you have virtually to step forward on your right foot and thrust the board forward. The stronger the wind the more firmly and forcibly do you thrust with your front foot.

So, to get the board moving:

- Hold the rig with your mast hand alone
- Pull the mast to windward past your shoulder
- Catch hold of the boom with your sheet hand
- Slowly sheet in the sail

Stopping is the easiest thing in the world. You want to stop? Just ease out the sail with your sheet hand, but slowly. Wind pressure and sail force decrease, the board will continue moving through the water for a little way, and you can hold the rig just with your mast hand on the boom or by the uphaul until you are ready to start off again.

Some learners simply cannot get started when the wind is blowing just a little more strongly. They either find that the board is pointing dead into the wind the moment they have got the sail to fill with wind, or they find that the board insists on *luffing up* until it is head to wind. The inevitable result is always the same—you fall in. There are two different reasons why the board luffs towards the wind:

- You did not check your *mast abeam* position just before sheeting in. The sail was not blowing out at 90° to the board, that is you did not have the wind abeam. If the sail was pointing rather further aft it

The board moves off—and she is sailing!

means that the board was already pointing almost into the wind and you cannot start like this.

- You did not pull the mast far enough to windward with your mast hand when preapring to start. So, when you sheeted in the sail with your sheet hand, the centre area of the rig was too far aft. You should have checked that the boom was parallel to the water; not drooping down aft. A sailboard will only move straight when the *centre of effort* of the sail (CE) is vertically above the centre of *lateral resistance* of the hull and daggerboard in the water (CLR). If the CE is aft of the CLR the board will *luff up*, ie turn towards the wind, as is explained later in the chapter on theory of sailing. The cure is to pull the mast further to windward so that the rig will be raked further forward when the sheet hand hardens in the sail. Say to yourself '*mast to windward*', then '*rake the mast forward*'.

The best way to practice this is just to cover a short distance. Then ease out the sail with your sheet hand, let the boom flag free and the board will come to a stop. Then pick up speed again, sheeting in the sail with your sheet hand, go a short way and sheet out again. So, rather than covering a longer distance at one go first sail a series of short stages, using your sheet hand alone; sheet out (let go) and then catch hold of the boom again and sheet it. Obviously if you let go the boom with your mast hand each time and hold the rig with the uphaul you will then have to grasp the boom again when re-starting and pull the mast past your shoulder to windward with your mast hand too.

This is an effective way of making a habit of the correct technique, and also gives you time to recover from your attempts to balance, which is far from easy.

- *Check*: How far have you moved from your departure point? Sometime and somehow you have to get back there!

If you have mastered the art of turning, getting back will be no problem; after bringing your board to a halt just stand in the mast abeam position and you can confidently turn the board until the bow is pointing homewards. It does not matter whether you turn the board to right or to left, but the more choppy the sea the easier it will be to turn the bow towards the wind and waves rather than the stern.

Once you have succeeded in bringing your sailboard back to your starting point like this you can risk sailing a longer straight stretch, but make sure when you sail away from the shore that the board is always at right angles to the wind, and this is usually also parallel to the waves. This point of sailing is called a *beam reach*, and it is only when you beam reach in one direction that you can return in the opposite direction without difficulty, also on a beam reach and without having to sail close to the wind direction (*close-hauled*).

Sailing straight

To sail straight ahead you have to adjust the rig all the time, and this is the special knack of boardsailing, which leads to the technique needed later for planing at speed. As before, two things must be remembered—*mast rake* (masthand) and *sail trim* (sail hand).

The rig must be raked far enough forward to prevent the sailboard luffing up, that is turning towards the wind, but must not be raked too far or the board will turn away from the wind which is called bearing away. You steer a board by inclining the rig forward or aft as you have already discovered when learning how to turn the board. You therefore have to tilt the rig back and forth slightly all the time to keep the board on course and sailing straight ahead. This is the job of the mast hand.

The sail should then be sheeted in just enough so that it stops *lifting*, but no further. Lifting means that the sail is nearly flapping. The front edge of the sail *lifts* as a first warning that the sail is set to too fine an angle. Pull the sheet hand in slightly. The trim of your sail should be checked continuously, especially in fluky or gusty winds. If you are able to sheet out the

Different ways of holding the wishbone boom. *Top*: Overhand grip; *Centre*: Underhand grip; *Bottom*: One overhand, the other underhand.

sail a little without it immediately starting to lift you had sheeted it in too much before. The sail develops maximum power just before it starts to lift.

In light winds you can sheet in the sail, just as described, standing upright and will not need to push the board forward with your front foot. But keep your knees completely flexed like a spring so that the motion of the board caused by small waves is absorbed by your legs.

In the mast abeam position the mast joint is between your feet when starting off, but when sailing straight ahead with the wind abeam you should move both feet further aft, the back foot roughly at the aft end of the daggerboard trunk, the front foot just aft of the mast join. The wind pressure on the sail passes through the boom to your arms and body and is transmitted to the board when you push forward with your front foot. When the wind blows harder, you can brace your foot against the mast joint.

In moderate winds your front leg is always nearly straight while your back leg is bent. This is the classic sailboarder's position in such winds
continued on page 52

Three more methods of holding the boom. *Top*: One overhand, the other underhand; *Centre*: Using an elbow can rest the forearm; *Bottom*: Holding the boom under an armpit saves effort when close-hauled in strong winds.

Right: In light winds the sail can be balanced without using much body weight. A boardsailor is able to stand almost upright.

Above: The classic boardsailor's position in moderate winds. His front leg is almost fully stretched to transmit to the board all the drive produced by the sail.

Right: In stronger winds the boardsailor has to use the weight of her body to balance the pull of the sail on the boom. Here she is hanging right under the sail close over the water. Much of the extraordinary appeal of boardsailing is due to the feeling of close sympathy with wind and waves.

which can be seen in the photographs. You cannot then counter the pull of the sail by just standing on the board and so must lean out against the wind, hanging on the boom. To start with you may pay for it with a fall but you will begin to look more like the expert boardsailors in the photographs who appear to hang there quite relaxed while planing effortlessly over the water. It is being so close to the water, in such close contact with wind and waves, that fascinates so many boardsailors. Obviously hanging out like this takes some courage, and many attempts will end with a ducking, but once you have practised enough and have found out how well your feet can control the board you will have taken a great step forward.

If your board starts to bury its nose, move both feet further aft to shift your weight nearer the stern. In a few rare cases your board may continue to behave like a submarine and even a considerable or extreme shift of weight will not stop it nosediving. If this happens continually the only sad conclusion is poor design. Your board has not been properly developed so you should change to another make as quickly as possible.

- So, to sail a straight course after getting under way:
  stand upright and straight at the hips and absorb the board's motion through your legs, like a skier on a bumpy piste. Your front foot is aft of the mast joint, your back foot at the aft end of the daggerboard trunk. The mast is upright when seen from ahead and you move the rig continuously with both arms, the mast hand keeping the mast raked at the right angle, (steering), and the sheet hand keeping the sail trimmed correctly, (power). When the wind freshens you lean back against it and thrust the board forward with your legs.

Naturally one cannot expect to become an expert overnight. These movements will only become automatic if you practise a great deal in all suitable conditions. Until you reach the automatic stage keep repeating to yourself:

- Getting under way—mast to windward.
- Sailing straight—the mast hand steers, the sheet hand controls power.

A common beginner's mistake occurs when he cannot hold the rig against a gust while standing upright and is pulled irresistably to leeward. In an effort to get back he bends at the waist. You know the reason because

A sudden gust or bearing away, will quickly pull the boardsailor into this unstable backside-out position.

Reacting to a gust.
1. Only the sheet hand should be eased out.

2. If a gust strikes and is too strong to counter extend your sheet arm until the sail spills wind and the pressure eases. Never relax your mast hand.

3. When the gust eases harden the sail with your sheet hand.

4. If the gust eases very suddenly sheet in hard and use the reaction to pull yourself back into balance.

you have met this backside-out stance already when you practised on land. Your mast arm in particular is at full stretch and you cannot use your weight or the thrust of your leg to counter the pull, nor can you use any strength because your hips are bent. Unless the gust eases you fall forward into the sail.

The correct technique is to ease the sheet hand slightly as soon as the pressure of the wind on the sail becomes excessive, but at the same time keep the mast arm well bent under all circumstances, and pull the mast further to windward in stronger winds.

If the gust eases slowly and gradually, harden in the sail with your sheet hand to match. If the wind drops rather suddenly and threatens to dump you backwards into the water, pull in the sail sharply. The sudden increase in pressure on the sail enables you to jerk yourself back by the boom and to regain your balance.

Important: use the sheet hand all the time because this controls the pressure of the sail. The more you sheet in, the greater the pressure; the more you sheet out, the less the pressure. The mast hand remains near your shoulder keeping the boom at the same level all the time and so is responsible for controlling the steering.

Luffing up and bearing away

You know now that the key to keeping a straight course is the mast rake. Conversely, altering the rake causes the board to change course.

When raising the sail from the water the board reacts by turning immediately if the uphaul is not led directly over the joint. When practising turning you made use of this fact and inclined the mast forward or aft with the sail shaking to make the board turn. You can help turning by pushing with your feet.

When getting under way you found that your board luffed up uncontrollably if you had not raked the mast far enough forward. Now you only need to reverse this notion to discover the secret of steering your sailboard. Remember:

- Rake the mast *aft* towards the stern and your sailboard will *luff up* towards the wind.
- Rake the mast *forward* towards the bow and the sailboard will *bear away* from the wind.

This is why a sailboard does not need a rudder like conventional sailing boats. It is all a question of the relationship between the centre of effort (CE) and the centre of lateral resistance (CLR), as has already been mentioned in connection with getting under way. In this section on practical boardsailing we are only concerned with how to sail; the reason why will be explained fully in the chapter on the theory of sailing.

The way to *luff up* is as follows: Start by sailing straight ahead on a beam reach, parallel to the waves with the wind blowing at right angles to the board. When you want to luff up incline the mast well towards the stern and shift your weight firmly onto your back foot, pushing your board into the turn. The rig must stay upright all the time (when viewed from ahead). The sail has to be sheeted in progressively in order to keep it full of wind without lifting.

Be decisive when luffing up and rake the mast aft firmly but only keep it there briefly while you are actually

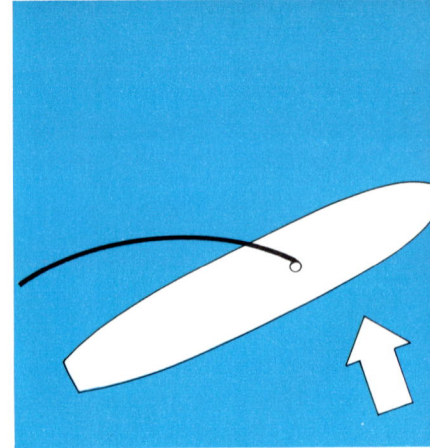

Luffing up. 1. Sailing straight ahead on a beam reach, the sail is correctly sheeted half way out and the mast is raked slightly forward.

altering course. Then return it to its former position raked slightly forward, although you will find it needs to be slightly less raked than when you were on a beam reach. You are now sailing at a closer angle to the wind than before. If you leave the mast raked aft the board will continue to turn and luff until it is head to wind where it will stop with sails shaking. Nobody can sail directly into the wind. The closest one can go with the sail full of wind is at an agnle of about 45° to the wind. This is called *close-hauled*, or on the wind. So to *luff*:

■ Rake the mast aft, sheet in the sail, put your weight on the back foot.

The way to *bear away* is as follows: Again start on a beam reach, sailing parallel to the waves with the wind abeam. When you want to bear away rake the mast sharply forwards to-

2. To luff up rake the rig aft and sheet in the sail. The white arrows show the true wind direction.

3. The more you rake the rig aft the quicker the board turns towards the wind. She pulls the sail across the stern of the board and pushes with her back foot to turn the board.

4. Finally the board continues luffing until it is here seen head to wind and the sail is shaking.

Bearing away

1. The board is close-hauled and the sail sheeted in. The mast is raked slightly forward.

2. To bear away she rakes the rig well forward.

3. In light winds the forward rake has to be very pronounced.

wards the bow, shift your weight onto your front foot and force the bow of the board round firmly so that it turns away from the wind. Again the rig must stay upright when viewed from ahead. As you bear away the sail has to be eased out progressively with the sheet hand to the point where it just stops lifting, and you will then be sailing on a broad reach with the wind free. When bearing away, the pull on the sail and the board speed both increase very suddenly and the board quickly starts to speed over the water—at any rate in fresher winds. You have to anticipate the increased wind pressure on the sail, bracing yourself firmly on the board with your front foot and leaning backwards to prevent the sail pulling you forward over the board and into the water—a typical catapult fall!
So, to *bear away*:

■ Rake the mast forward, sheet out the sail and brace yourself firmly on the board with your front leg.

Luffing up and bearing away can easily be practised by just following a wavy course. Start from the mast abeam position and sail a short way straight ahead with the wind abeam, then luff slightly and sail close-hauled; now bear away, first to a beam reach and then further to a broad reach; luff again until you are back on a beam reach and so on.

You can make this much more interesting by using objects such as mooring buoys, other boats or a wandering shore line to provide good reasons for altering course.

Remember again the two points:

■ To luff up rake the mast aft.
■ To bear away rake the mast forward.

4. Only with a lot of mast rake will the board turn away from the wind. The sail is then sheeted out.

5. The board is back on a beam reach and the mast can be returned to its normal position for sailing straight, raked slightly forward.

and absorb them so thoroughly that your actions become automatic. You will be astonished at how accurately you can steer your sailboard and how easily you can work your way between moving objects such as other boardsailors. For safety bear in mind how far your mast will reach when it falls and keep at least one mast length away.

Running before the wind

If you bear away further from a broad reach you will be sailing downwind, or running before the wind moving in the same direction as the waves. You will no longer be standing on the side of the board but centrally with the daggerboard between your feet. You can only see where you are going through the window in the sail, which is right in front of you, because you have sheeted it out until it is setting at right angles to the board. The mast is raked well to one side and the boom points upwards sharply. On a sailboard, running is a very unstable course because you have to balance yourself with your feet only across the width of the board instead of along its length. Steering, on the other hand, is no problem; when you rake the rig to the right the board will turn to the left, tilt it to the left and the board will turn right.

The daggerboard serves no purpose on a run because you sail in the same direction as the wind blows and therefore make no leeway. In stronger winds particularly it is best to raise the daggerboard half way or take it right out and hang it over your sail arm where it interferes least with your mobility.

The sole difficulty when running downwind is balance, and practice is the only answer. Expertise comes simply as a result of experience.

Left: *Running*. This is the most unstable point of sailing and therefore the least popular as well as being the slowest. The sail is at right angles to the board and you can only see forward through the window in the sail.

Below: Running in more wind can be quite difficult and will be discussed later. One has to lean aft and be very sensitive to sheet adjustment.

The sailing terms

Head to wind
A boardsailor describes the direction in which his board moves by relating it to the direction of the wind and not to the way the shore runs. Head to wind means that the board just points into the wind and the sail shakes free and is parallel to it. No progress can be made in this direction.

Close-hauled, or on a tack
You can sail at an angle of about 45° to the wind with the sail full of wind and fairly close to the centre line. Because the leeway component of the sail's total power is high you can only make progress forwards because the daggerboard discourages the board from moving sideways. Only a small component of the total power is in the forward direction and so this is a relatively slow point of sailing.

Sailing to windward, or beating
You cannot sail straight to an objective to windward but, because you can sail close-hauled at 45° to the right and left of windward, you can zigzag your way to a point dead to windward. This is also called beating to windward.

Beam reach
If you bear away until the wind blows at 90° to the board, which then sails parallel to the waves, the wind is said to be abeam and you are sailing on a beam reach. The sail is sheeted out half way, the board moves considerably faster because the forward component is high, and only half the daggerboard is required.

Broad reach
When you bear away further the wind blows at an angle from aft and the board is said to be broad reaching. This is the fastest point of sailing. The sail is sheeted out a long way and is almost at right angles to the board so the force is almost all acting forwards. The daggerboard is barely necessary because the board sails almost in the same direction as the wind blows.

Running
If you bear away from a broad reach until the wind blows from dead astern you are said to be running or on a run. This is a relatively slow point of sailing for technical aerodynamic reasons. The board is very unstable, and can be very difficult in strong winds. The sail is exactly ahead of you at right angles to the board and you can only see forward through the window. The daggerboard only slows the board slightly and has no other purpose.

Changing tacks

Gradually you begin to enjoy the real pleasure of boardsailing. Once you are reasonably steady on the board and can luff up and bear away to sail on different courses you do not have to sail straight all the time but can sail wherever you wish.

You will certainly have discovered that some refinements are missing. Even when sailing back and forth on a straight course you had to stop and turn the board slowly round so that you could return with your sail on the opposite side.

When the sail sets to port and the wind blows from the starboard side the sailor says he is on *starboard tack*; with the sail to starboard and the wind from the port side he is on *port tack*. Port is the nautical term for left and starboard is the term for right when facing in the direction of forward motion.

Up to now you have managed to change the direction in which you sail by turning your board so that the sail is set on the opposite side of the board, in other words you have changed tacks. This is a sure method but far too slow for an expert boardsailor, and far too clumsy! The board has to be stopped completely, turned right round and then restarted all of which is particularly wasteful when beating to windward because you only need to turn through 90° and want to lose as little as possible of the distance that you have gained to windward.

An alternative method of changing tacks, often simply called *tacking*, is to luff up into the wind, turn the bow past the wind direction and bear away onto a close-hauled course on the opposite tack. The sail shakes as the board passes through the head to wind attitude. As the board turns further the sail moves over to the opposite side while you change sides by stepping around forward of the mast. You then sail away on the new tack.

Naturally you have to change your handholds and grip to the other side of the wishbone boom when you change tacks, but that is not difficult; it just needs practice. The difference between turning the board and tacking is that when you turn the board it swivels round on the spot while the sail shakes all the time whereas, when tacking, you sail the board round an arc keeping the sail full of wind, and so the sail shakes only briefly as you pass head to wind. When turning on the spot use your feet to push the board round, but when tacking you use the momentum of the board's forward motion to swing it past the 'dead sector' when the sail is not developing any power. This is the only way to overcome the period when the sail is head to wind, at which point the wind cannot drive the board forward.

A learner also finds it hard to keep his balance during the stage when the bows are passing through the eye of the wind. Instead of holding the boom against the wind pressure on the sail, which gives good support, he is just holding the uphaul. The quicker one changes sides and continues sailing the sooner can one benefit from the steadying effect of the wind on the sail. Take particular note of these two points when practising:

make the board swing round quickly and keep the unstable period as short as possible.

Before learning to tack you must be able to sail close-hauled, luff up and bear away, as well as knowing how to turn the board in case you do not succeed in getting it to swing round far enough during tacking.

So this is how to change tacks: You are sailing close-hauled, let us say on port tack. The sail is to starboard, you are on the port side of the board, your left hand is your mast hand and your right is the sheet hand.

Rake the mast aft to luff up and, at the same time, shift your weight firmly onto the back leg, pushing the stern of the board into the turn to encourage the bow to swing round more easily. The board then curves up into the wind and the sail starts to shake. As soon as the pressure of the wind on the sail eases, your sheet hand can release the boom and take hold of the uphaul. As the board turns you shuffle round forward of the mast, and your mast hand also grasps the uphaul. At this point you will be standing virtually in the same position relative to the sail as mast abeam, except that the board is pointing into the wind and turning onto the new tack instead of lying at right angles to the wind.

You must now make use of your momentum to get under way again on the new tack by stepping further round the mast to the starboard side and grasping the boom with your right hand, which is now the mast hand. Release the uphaul with your left hand, which becomes the sheet hand, pull the rig to windward with your mast hand, as you have learnt, sheet in the sail with your left hand and you will already be under way again.

Everything depends on the swing which must be enough to carry the board round from one tack to the other, preferably without coming to a stop, and the method of generating swing is simply to luff up firmly and to bear away equally firmly. Luffing up to tack must be accentuated, perhaps exaggerated, with the mast raked so far aft that the boom is almost touching the water. Sheet the sail in firmly with your sheet hand—you can even *back* the sail by pulling it beyond the board's centreline to accelerate the turning motion. The moment that the board has swung through the eye of the wind you exaggerate the action of bearing away just as much by inclining the mast extremely far forward. As soon as the board has started to move on the new tack you return the mast to its normal close-hauled position.

What does one do if the board will not bear away after tacking? The sail may be full of wind on the new tack although the board has not swung round completely. The answer is to pull the sail back beyond the centreline and to use your feet. Sheet in the sail fully with your sheet hand and simultaneously thrust the bow away from the wind forcibly with your front foot, but remember to have your front foot forward of the mast.

Each time you tack, the sheet and mast hands exchange duties. This routine needs practice and so the more you sail, the sooner will you be able to do it all automatically.

Initially you are sure to find that you have not enough swing to carry the board through the 'dead' sector and onto the new tack. The board will come to a stop but that will not matter because, knowing how to turn, you can easily get the board back to the mast abeam position and start again. The art of tacking is not absolutely essential, because you can make a turn on the spot instead. But tacking, especially when quick, makes sailing to windward much easier, and it is particularly then that you do not want to loose distance gained to windward by drifting to leeward again as you laboriously turn the board round.

An aspect of boardsailing that gives great satisfaction is that your method of changing tacks can always be matched to the limit of your skill. As a beginner you just turn the board round, as an advanced beginner you use a turn only when you fail to tack properly and, as an expert boardsailor you use the tack just described even if, in strong winds you may still have to fall back on the spot turn and spend a few moments in the mast abeam position before starting again. Racing boardsailors do not normally shuffle slowly round the mast but change sides with one quick jump as described later under the *jump tack*. The Gold Medal for elegance goes to the free style competition boardsailor who throws the sail round in one powerful swing and sails away on the opposite tack without a break.

There are very many styles of tacking so it is up to you to choose the way that suits you best. You should be able to look back on your first complete success after an hour or two of practice.

Changing tacks

1.
2.
3.
4.
5.
6.
7.

In this series of photos the boardsailor starts from a beam reach on port tack (1). He rakes the mast well aft to luff up and starts to sheet in the sail (2). The board starts to turn. He rakes the mast further aft to accelerate the swing (3). Now the board turns very quickly. His feet have not changed their position on the board (4). He accelerates the swing by pulling the sail back across the centreline. The board turns until it is almost head to wind. The wind pressure in the sail eases and it starts to shake (5). Finally the board is head to wind and the whole sail is shaking. The boardsailor has let go of the boom and holds the rig with the uphual (6). He steps round forward of the mast (7). The board must be kept swinging, even though the sail is shaking, so that it can get to the new mast abeam position and be got moving again (8). Move to the new windward side and turn the board further round. He has reached the mast abeam position (9). Now he gets under way as usual. The new mast hand grasps the boom and pulls the mast to windward (10). The new sheet hand grasps the boom and sheets in the sail. The board sails off on starboard tack (11).

Gybing

Once you have learnt to gybe you will be fully manoeuvrable. Not only can you speed over the water in any direction, as we promised when introducing tacking, but you can sail in circles and figures of eight, apparently regardless of the direction of the wind.

Gybing means altering course from a broad reach or a run by bearing away until the stern crosses the wind direction. The sail is allowed to swing forward over the bow to fill again on the opposite side. Unlike tacking, when the boardsailor has to step or jump round forward of the mast, he stays standing above the daggerboard trunk during a gybe. Gybing from a broad reach involves altering course about 90° but when running, the board only turns a few degrees.

With the wind dead aft it matters little whether the sail is set to the right of left of the board; it will be at right angles to the centreline whether the mast tip points to port or to starboard. You might think it difficult to decide whether the sailboard is on port tack or starboard tack when running, but the rule given earlier still holds good if you remember which side the sail is set.

Suppose that you are reaching on starboard tack and bear away until you are running dead before the wind. The sail will lie across the board with the boom pointing to port and the mast pointing to starboard.

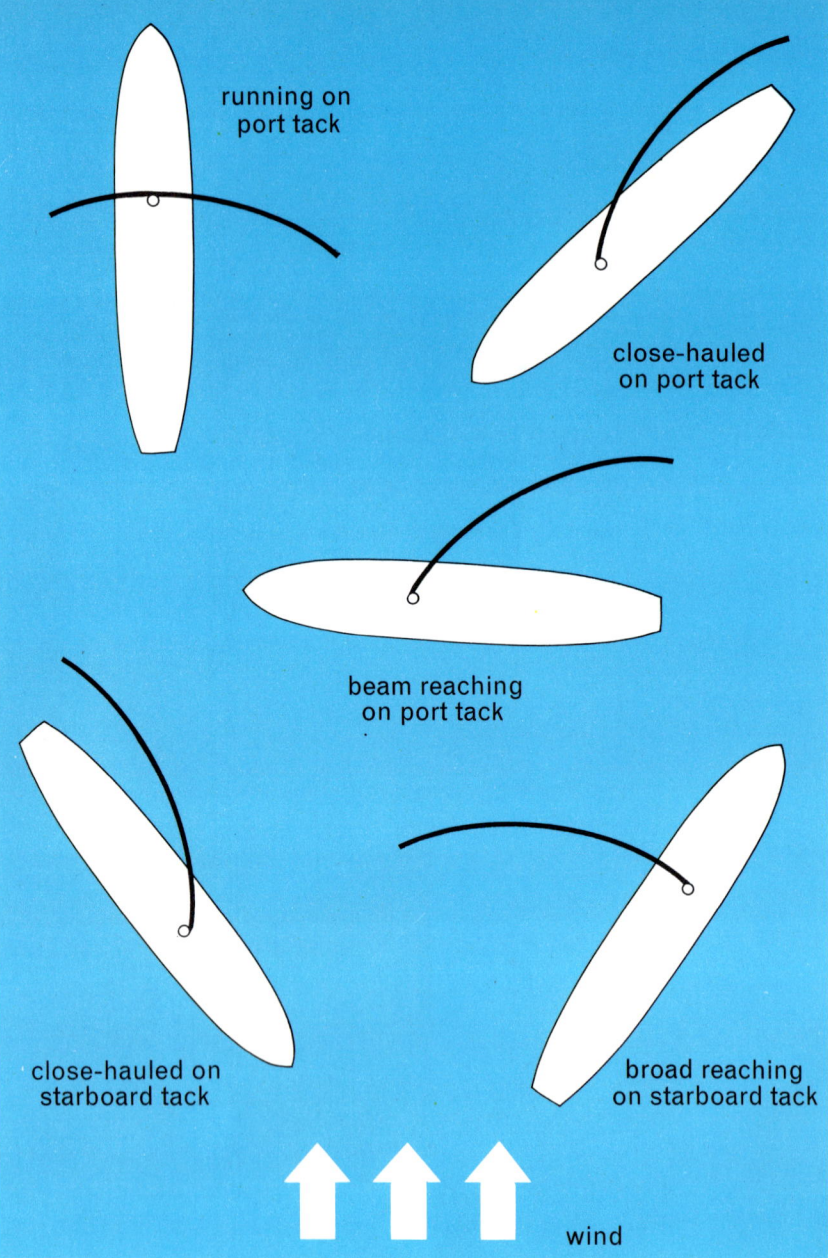

When sailing on port tack, the wind comes over the port side. The sail is to starboard. On starboard tack the wind comes over the starboard side. The sail is to port.

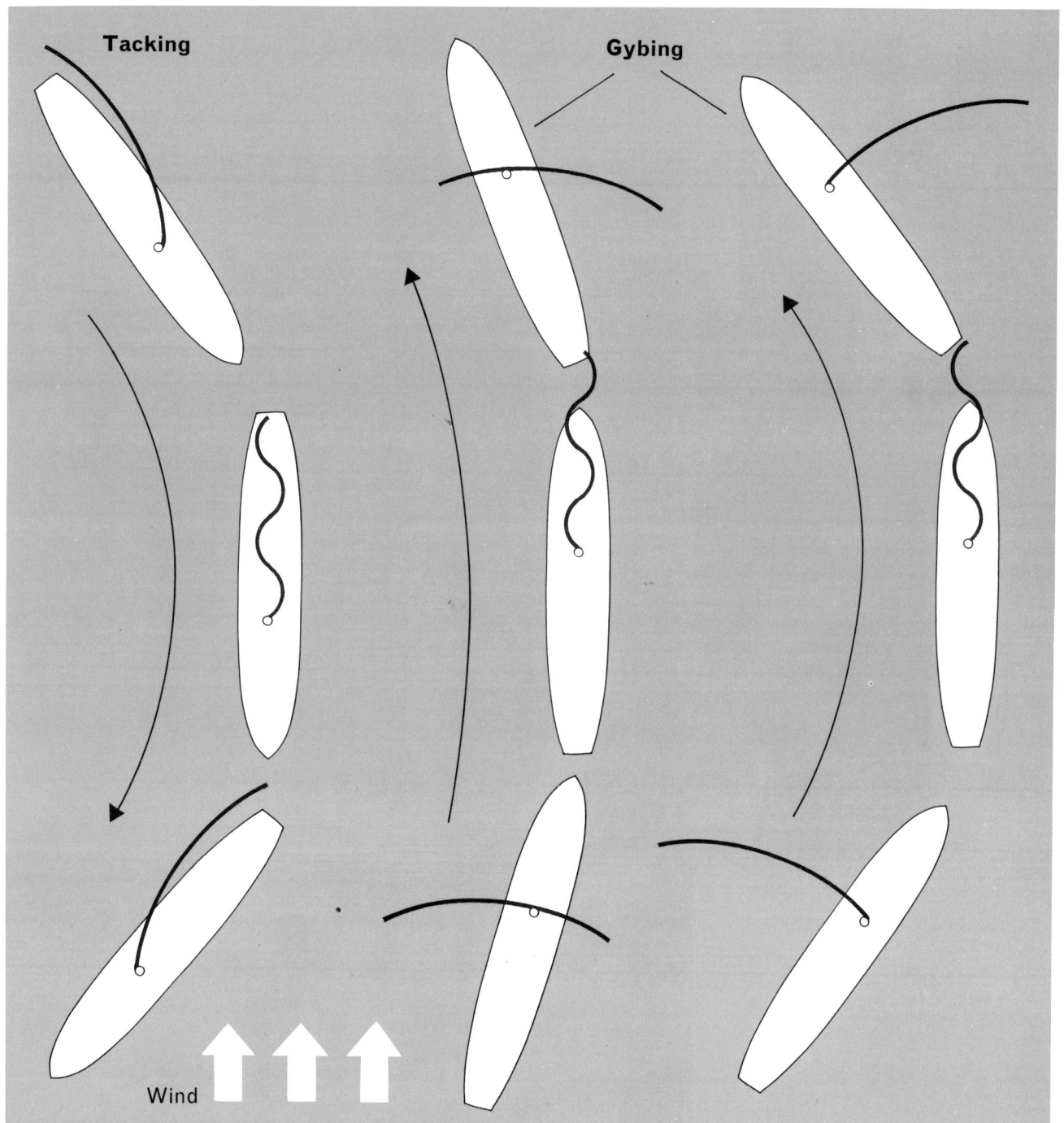

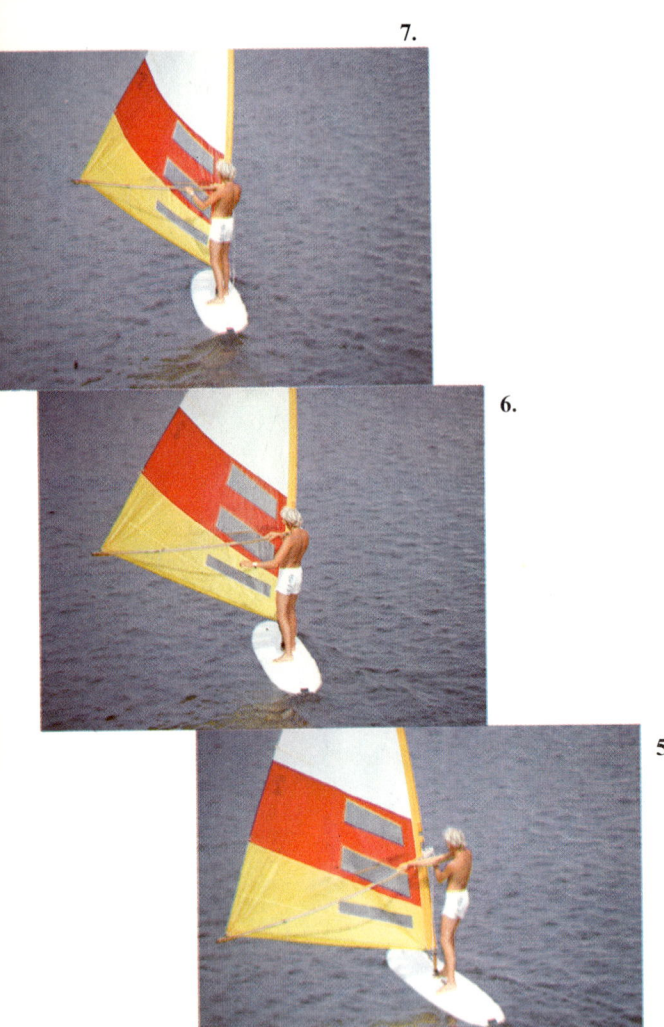

Gybing

The board is being gybed from a broad reach on port tack to a broad reach on starboard tack. Start on port tack with the sail sheeted well out (1). He rakes the rig forward and to windward by stretching out his mast arm and bears away on to a running course. The wind is so light that he has already taken hold of the uphaul with his mast hand (2). As soon as his sheet hand releases the boom the wind blows the sail forward (3). He accelerates the swing by pulling the rig to starboard with his left hand which sends the sail to port and helps the board to continue turning (4). Now he must catch the boom quickly because the sail is already half full of wind as a result of his having swung it over. His right hand becomes the mast hand and reaches over to grasp the boom (5). His left hand drops the uphaul to become the sheet hand (6). He grips the boom further from the mast, sheeting in the sail as far as necessary for sailing a broad reach on the new starboard tack (7).

You will still be on starboard tack until the moment you swing the sail onto the opposite side. You will then have gybed onto port tack. So, when running:

- If the mast points to starboard you are on starboard tack.
- If the mast points to port you are on port tack.

This is particularly important because of giving way to other sailing boats or sailboards when complying with the *right-of-way rules* and, of course, with the special *racing rules* when you are racing. More details are given later.

The gybe is learnt last because first you have to be able to sail a broad reach, be reasonably steady when running, be able to turn the board, and be able to sail to windward too because, whenever you sail downwind, you later have to work back to windward again.

First try gybing from a running course rather than from a braod reach because this avoids the extra problems of balance when bearing away. This is how to do it: You are sailing on a run, probably rather unsteadily, say on port tack (with the mast raked to port). Your mast hand is therefore your left hand and your sail hand your right. In principle all you have to do is to let the whole rig swing forward over the bow and pull it round until it is in virtually the same position on the opposite side (but with the mast raked to starboard). Your right and left hands will have exchanged duties as mast and sheet hands in the same way as they do when you tack.

So you are sailing your board exactly downwind. Then bear away slighty more. Release the boom with your right or sheet hand and catch hold of the uphaul. The wind immediately blows the sail forward over the bow and you can release the boom to grasp the uphaul with your masthand too. You can speed up the swing of the sail by briefly pulling the whole rig to starboard with your right hand, the former sheet hand. Your right hand now becomes the new mast hand and reaches over the left to grasp the boom. Your left hand can then release the uphaul and catch hold of the boom to sheet in the sail to its normal running position on the other tack. The board keeps moving naturally the whole time.

The boom should not swing over jerkily; a relatively gentle tug on the uphaul very effectively throws the sail straight into your hands on the opposite side and largely avoids the need to sheet in the sail with your sheet hand.

In light winds practise gybing repeatedly at frequent intervals using this gentle swinging action each time and altering course as little as possible. After every gybe get the board and rig perfectly balanced and steady before you throw the sail over again.

Note: Re-set the rig on the new tack fast and rake the mast well

1.

2.

because otherwise the board will luff up very rapidly to a broad reach or even to a beam reach as you sheet in the sail.

Watch out in stronger winds! You will speed away immediately the sail fills. The sudden tug of the sail can pull you right off your feet and catapult you forward into the water. Especially when gybing from one broad reach to the other it is therefore vital to place your feet correctly to anticipate this sudden tug from the sail. Brace yourself ready for the new tack and you will find that after some practice you can gybe from a broad reach too.

Sailing round a circle

Once you have mastered the art of gybing and tacking you can alter course as you wish, regardless of whether the wind is ahead or free. The 'dead sector', 45° on either side of the wind direction, is still, of course, unattainable. You can nevertheless now sail a complete circle as is taught in boardsailing schools. To those who do not understand about sailing, the boardsailor seems to be able to sail anywhere independent of wind direction when doing this exercise. A neat trick can disguise the existence of this dead sector.

A typical catapult fall. He could not hold the sudden pull as the sail filled in a gust. This can also happen when bearing away to a beam or broad reach. The pull of the sail catapults him over the board and into the water.

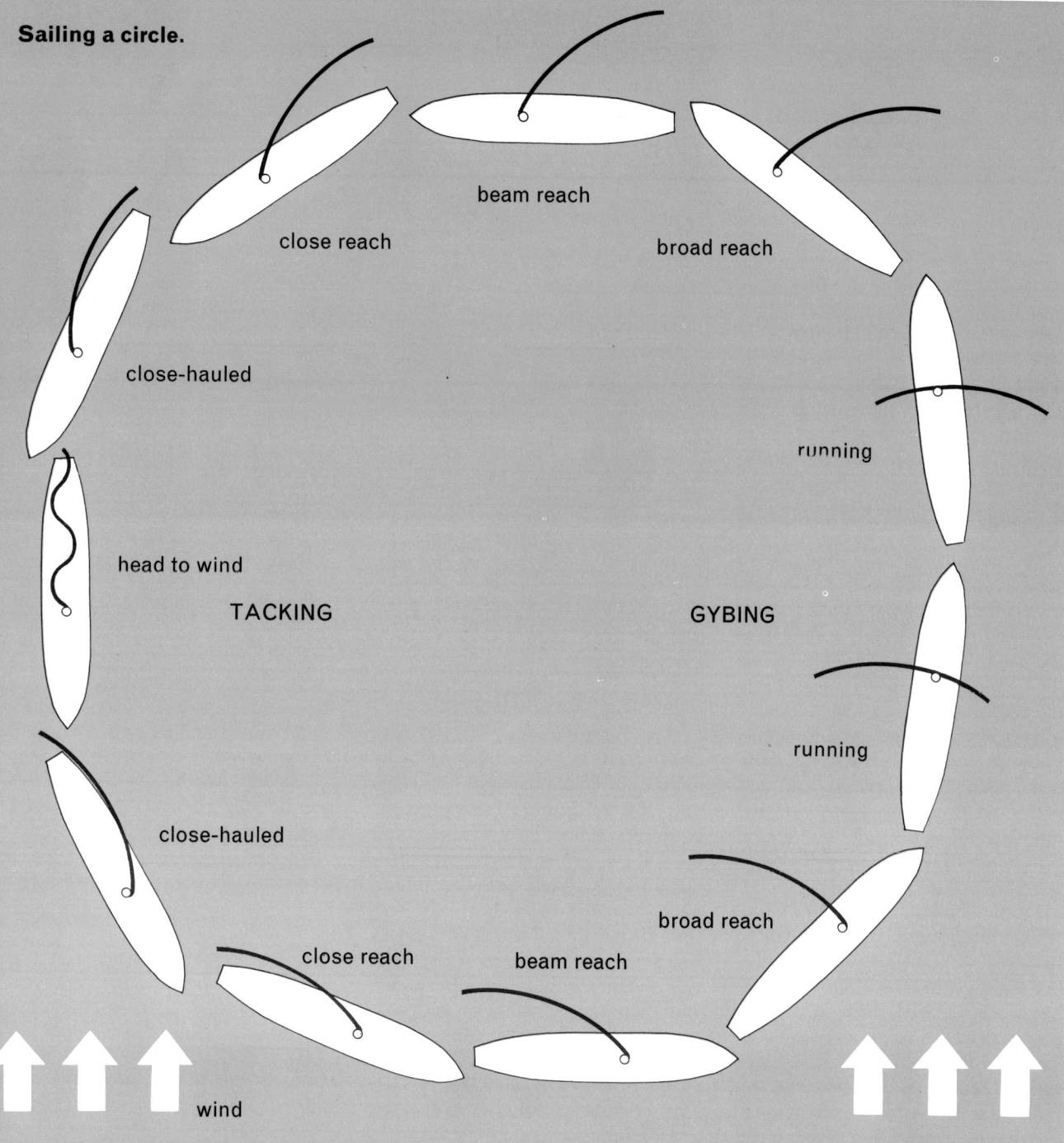

Falling

As we near the end of this basic instruction course you should learn how to fall correctly. Boardsailing and falling are as inseparable as bread and butter. Falling is an inevitable and normal consequence of a boardsailor on his way to becoming an expert. Nothing ventured is nothing won. You cannot learn or improve your technique without risking a fall.

Just as with judo you should learn how to fall correctly, and the right way to fall will avoid injuring yourself or damaging the sail or the rest of the gear. Whenever possible fall on the opposite side to the sail and into the water which is not hard like the board. For example, you generally know in advance that you are about to be catapulted forward, and it is better to drop the boom at that moment and let the rig crash forward or to leeward while you splash backwards neatly into the water.

Do not panic if you fall to windward with the whole rig above you so that when you surface you find yourself underneath the sail. Stretch your hands above your head—which is a protective reflex action anyway—and feel your way to the luff or leech of the sail where you can emerge and pull yourself back to the board. There is no need to dive deeply to get clear of the rig, and this would be unnecessarily exhausting. It is a mistake also to clamber back onto the board and immediately rush to raise the sail out of the water again. This merely tenses your muscles, affects your mobility and prevents you from being relaxed which is so essential for good balance. First pull yourself quietly back onto the board and then wait a while to get your breath back, sitting in the comfortable resting position with your feet on the board or in the water. Watch your friends or other boardsailors and—relax.

The sail will drop on top of this falling boardsailor who is automatically holding up his hands to protect himself. The rig generally drops quite gently, cushioned by the air beneath it.

Relaxing. The rig is floating in the water while the boardsailor rests on his board. The sailboard is the only sailing craft that allows you to do this.

Relaxation

Every beginner creeps home feeling stiff all over after his first hours of boardsailing! This is caused more by general body tension, added to uncertainty and, perhaps, anxiety rather than by too much effort. As soon as you have learnt how to get under way and can sail some distance you will discover that your forearms become cramped and painful. The following advice will certainly help.

Take a rest from time to time! Lower the rig on the water and sit on the board for a few minutes. Shake your arms about and hold them above your head to let the blood circulate freely. Often you will feel small knots in your forearm muscles and you can massage these gently although they will take some time to disperse completely. The arms of a good wet suit should be cut with a wedge-shaped gusset to allow ample room at the cuffs and forearm and should not be tapered.

Go boardsailing often! Soon you will no longer need to rest because your finger and forearm muscles, which are little used in normal life, will have adjusted themselves to the new stresses.

The theory of sailing

How is it that a boat can sail towards the wind direction? If the wind presses on the sail surely it can only push it away. How can it pull a sailing boat or sailboard towards it?

Many boardsailors are content merely to know that the wind does in fact pull them forward and, as a start it can be better to learn by actually sailing the board. However a knowledge of how forces act on the sail and board is essential if the finer points of boardsailing technique are to be mastered. This knowledge will be needed in strong winds and particularly when racing. You need to understand just how your wind engine, the sail, actually works. In this book we started with practical sailing. Now we move on to theory and will then revert to more advanced practice.

First an astonishing but vital fact: the true wind that blows over land and sea is not the wind that drives you forward. The moment that a boat starts to move through the water an equal and opposite wind is felt on board due to her forward motion. It comes from directly ahead and combines with whatever other wind exists

The same laws of aerodynamics apply to sailboards as to sailing boats. Both can sail at an angle of about 45° to the wind direction and sometimes slightly closer. In this racing start number 1002 is not sailing as close to the wind as the others and so is losing distance to windward.

at that moment to form the *apparent wind* that is the actual wind which drives the boar.

The direction of the *true wind* can only be seen by observing its effect on stationary objects such as a flag on land, smoke from a chimney or a sail shaking on a board or boat that is lying motionless. It follows from this that, given a true wind that is constant in direction and strength, the faster a boat sails the more will the combination of the wind of motion and the true wind, (*the apparent wind*), change its direction to blow more from the boat's bow. This is why when a heavy, slow boat sailing on a beam reach with her sails full and the boom half way out, is passed by, say, a fast racing catamaran on the same course, the latter's sails will be trimmed almost as for a close-hauled course. In spite of this the sailing terms, close-hauled, beam reach, broad reach and running always relate to the true wind direction.

A sailor is able to luff up in a gust because, although the true wind component increases, the component due to boat speed is unchanged at first; the apparent wind therefore blows from further aft than before the gust.

But how is it that a sailing boat can move forwards at an angle of about 45° to the wind anyway? This is due to the camber or fullness of the sail. It is only on a dead run that the boat is thrust forward when the wind blows directly over the stern and on to the sail.

Sail power by push

A glance at the drawing of true wind and apparent wind when running makes it clear why the run is the slowest point of sailing. The wind arising from board speed blows in exactly the opposite direction to the true wind. So the apparent wind that results therefore blows less strongly than the true wind but from approximately the same direction. The diagram of air flow round a running sail shows that it is a *stalled* airfoil which has no smooth air flow over its surface and is surrounded by turbulence.

Sail power by pull

On all other points of sailing the wind blows into the leading edge of the sail at a small angle. The mast and sail

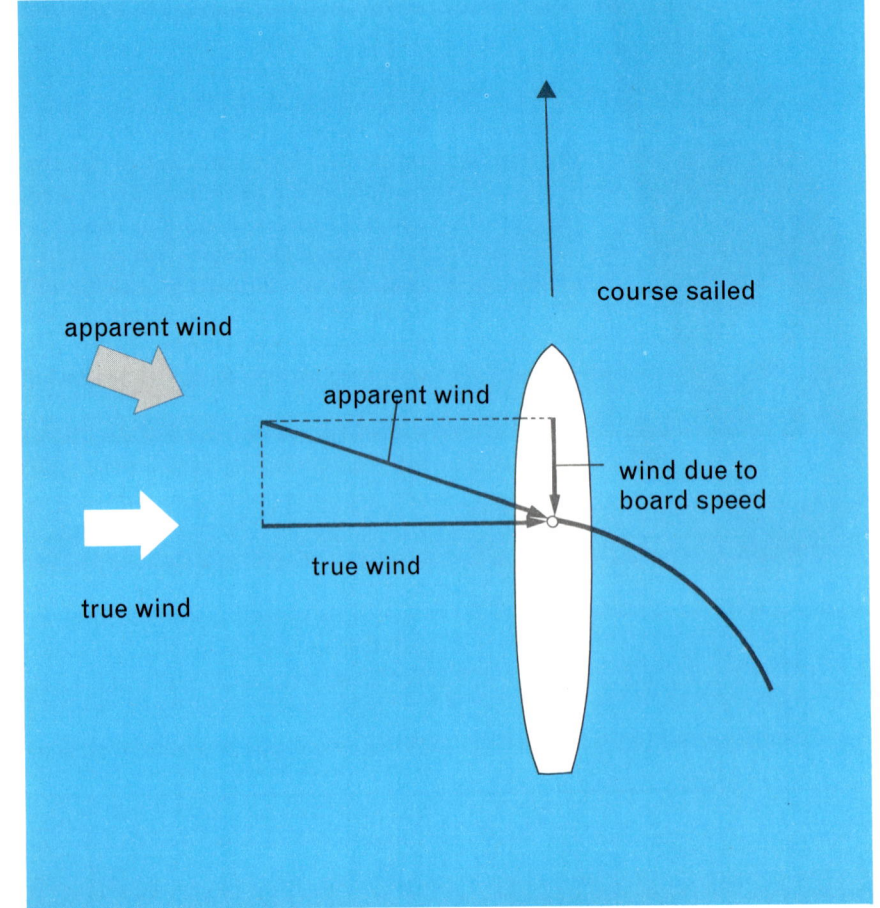

Sailing craft use the apparent wind for propulsion. This is the resultant of the true wind and the wind arising from the board's forward motion.

divide the air flow which streams along the sail to windward and leeward before converging aft of the leech. The stream-lines to windward are compressed and push the sail into a curve. To windward they are diverted by the curvature of the sail and have to travel further and hence to flow faster. This causes pressure to fall to leeward and, whenever there is a difference of pressure, air attempts to correct the difference by flowing to the low pressure area. Thus the sail cloth is also pulled out toward the leeward direction by suction, and this suction is much more powerful than the push from the windward sail. The sail is literally *pulled* approximately perpendicular to the boom angle taking the board and sailor with it.

However, with the sail set as described, and sheeted in close to the centre line the board would only be pulled a little ahead of dead to leeward. But the board has a daggerboard which reaches down into the water, making it virtually impossible for the sailboard to move

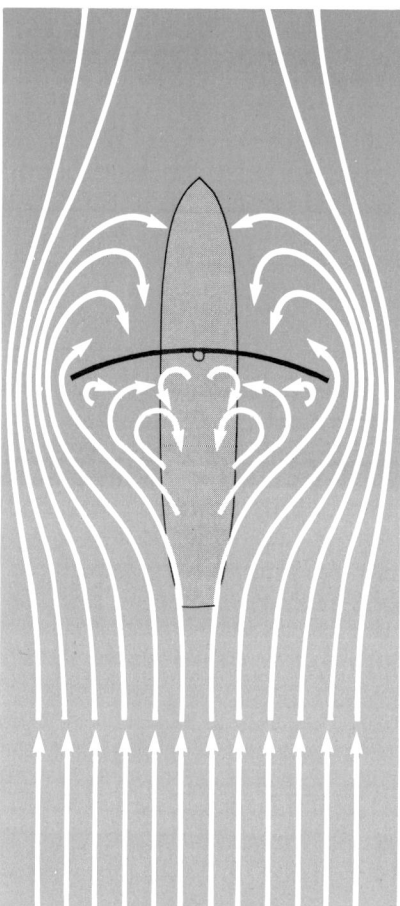

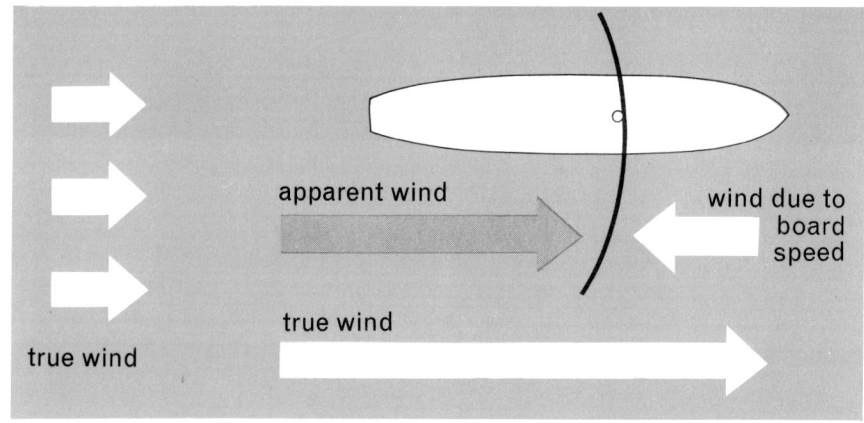

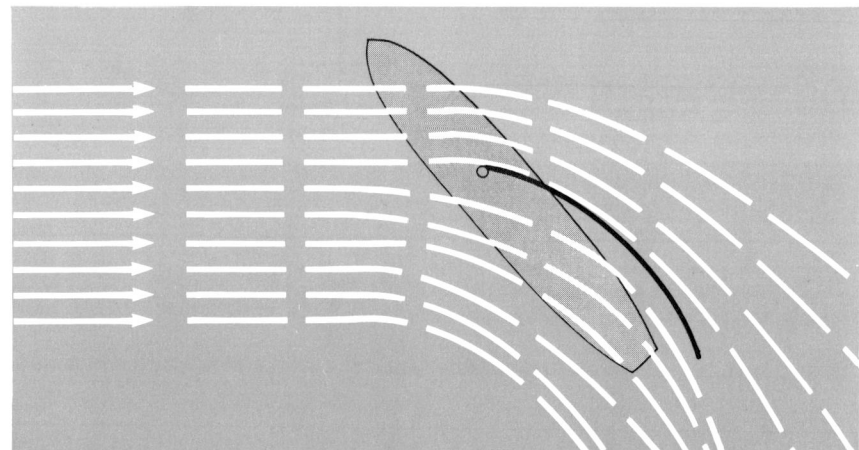

Above: Air flow round the sail when running before the wind.

Upper left: Calculating the apparent wind when running.

Lower left: Airflow over a sail. Pressure is high on the windward side of the sail but low on the leeward side and it is this which pulls the sail into its curved shape and hence pulls the boat too.

When sailing close-hauled only a small part of total wind force is converted into driving force.

sideways. The result is that the part of the total force produced by the sail which acts forward of the beam is converted into forward propulsion, and the large remainder is cancelled out by the pressure on the daggerboard and balanced by the boardsailor and rig hanging out to windward.

So a sailboard, and of course a sailing boat too, is propelled by push along, when running, whereas on all other courses, when air flow is laminar and streams over the sail, propulsion is mainly due to pull. The wind engine only functions because the sail is curved and because there is a daggerboard to counter the lateral or leeway force.

As an engine for propelling the board to windward the sailboard rig is rather inefficient! On a close-hauled course the driving force is least relative to the total force because the degree and direction of the total force differs little from that of the leeway force. This is why a sailboard is relatively slow when close-hauled. If the boardsailor pinches, that is if he sails extremely close to the wind direction, forward force almost disappears and, although the sail is full of wind, the board barely makes headway. The right compromise has to be found

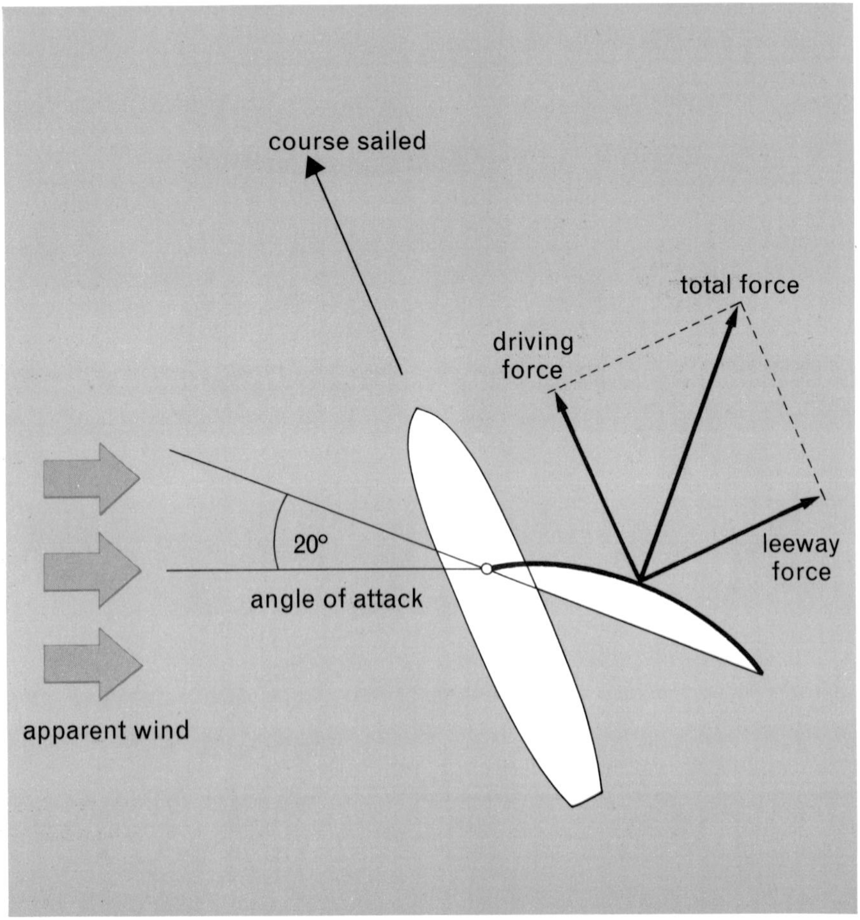

On a beam reach the total wind force acts more nearly towards the direction in which the board is sailing and so the side component is much smaller. So a sailing craft can move fast on a beam reach.

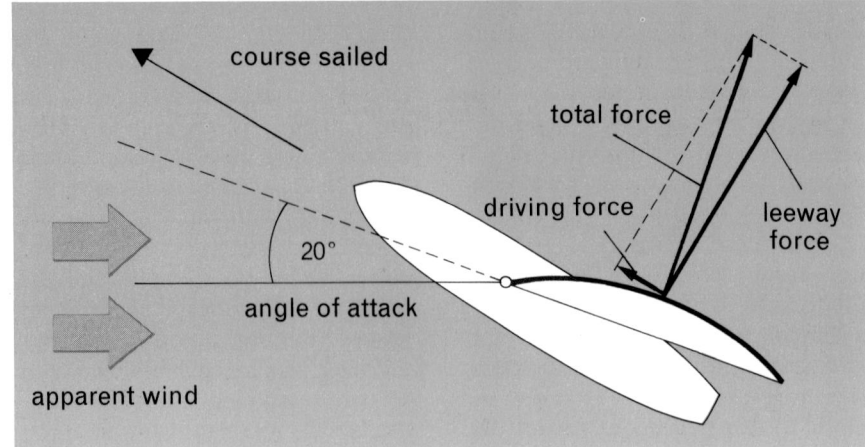

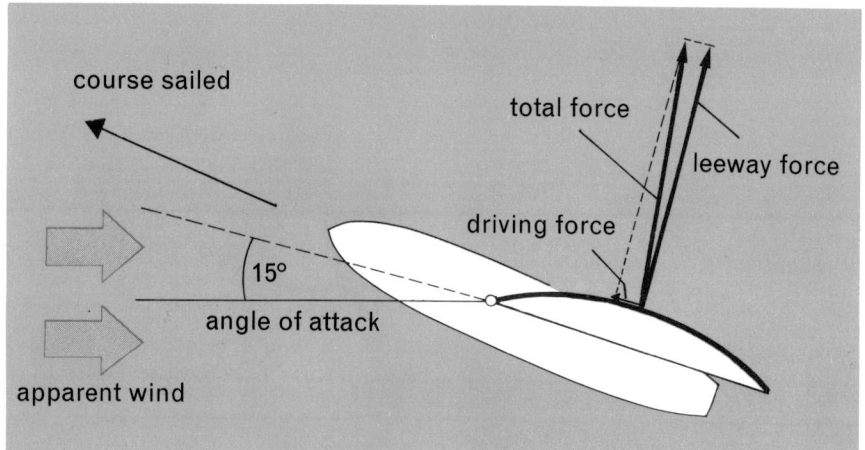

When the boardsailor pinches, that is when he steers the board too close to the wind direction and sheets the sail right in, the driving force component diminishes rapidly.

between board speed and the closest practicable angle to the wind direction.

Driving force is greatest in relation to total force when reaching because the leeway component is much smaller than the total force leaving a large component for propulsion. In any case total force is directed more forward due to the sail being eased out. It is hardly surprising that this is a faster direction of sailing.

The efficiency of the sail varies so much, depending on the direction of sailing, that it is all the more important to achieve maximum sail efficiency.

So, for best performance:

- The camber or draft of the sail must be aerodynamically efficient so as to produce the greatest difference in pressure.
- On every direction of sailing the sail must be trimmed to the correct angle of attack to the apparent wind.

Camber

The power of a sail varies with difference in pressure, and that means with the degree of fullness of the sail. There are practical limits however to

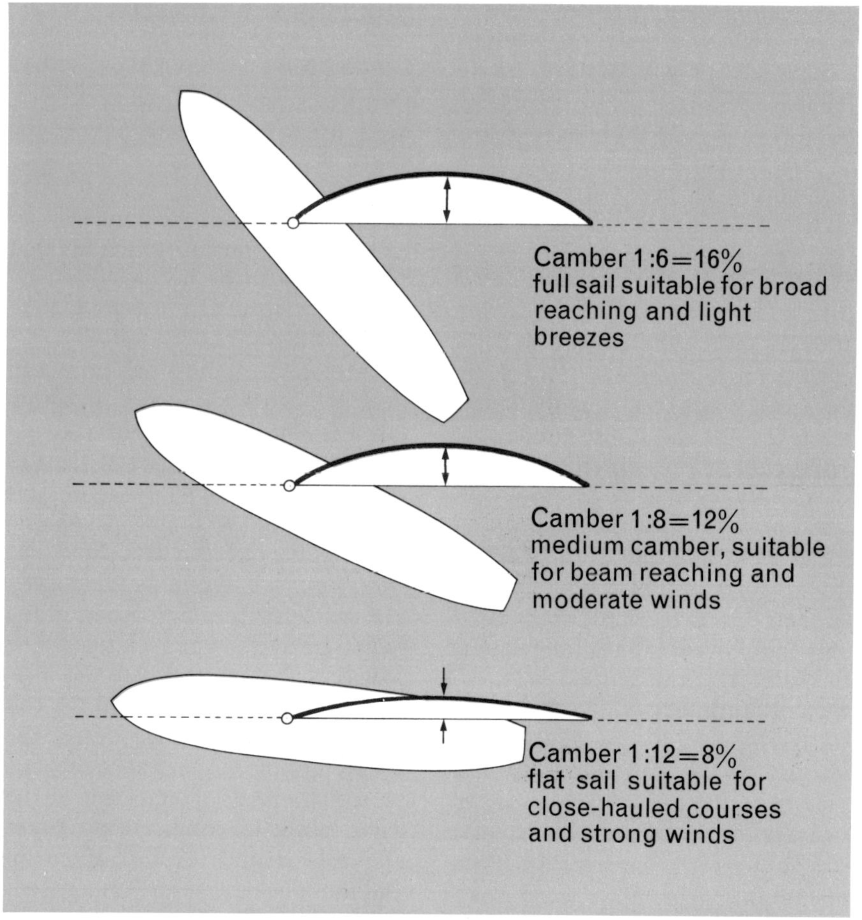

The camber or draft of the sail, that is its curvature, is the ratio of the greatest distance between the chord and the sail to the length of the chord.

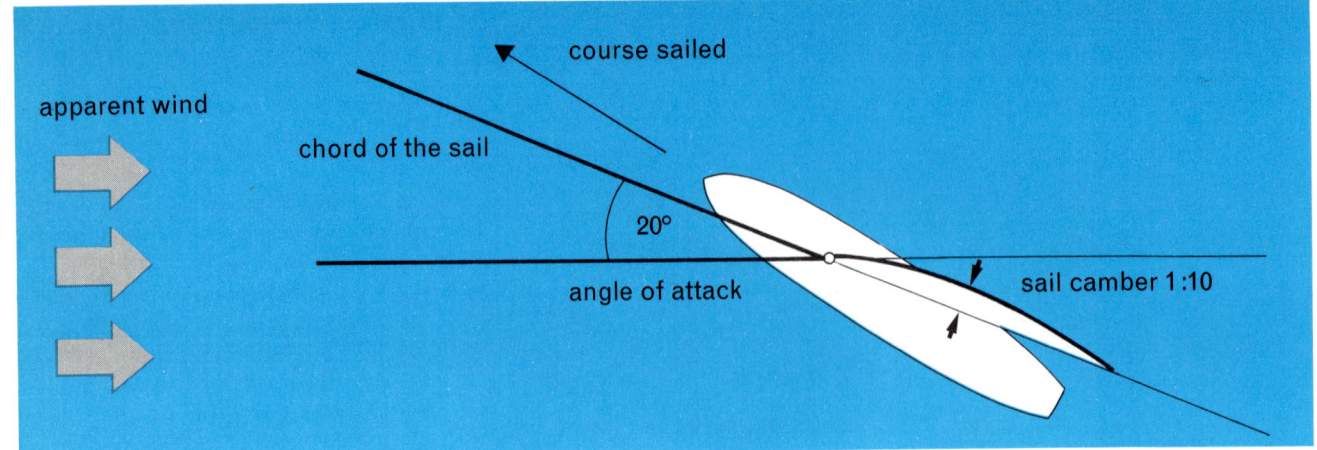

the fullness when wind speed increases and when sailing close-hauled. A board cannot be sailed close to the wind direction with a very full sail without the luff lifting, and if the sail was sheeted in more, the forward driving component would disappear altogether. The closer you want to sail to the wind, and the stronger the breeze, the flatter the sail should be. Conversely the lighter the breeze and the freer your course, the fuller the sail. A ratio of 1:7 (depth of Camber to length of Chord) is considered satisfactory for broad reaching in a moderate wind, force 3–4; much more, and the lee side airflow comes 'unstuck' and turbulent, and hence the power falls off.

Adjusting sail camber to match wind strength is called *sail tuning*. Unlike the crew of a racing boat a boardsailor rarely adjusts the fullness of his sail on different courses during a race because he has no spare hand available and would first have to come to a halt, thereby losing far more ground than he would gain by the greater speed resulting from adjusting the camber of the sail.

A poor or badly stretched sail can be seen to have its maximum camber too far aft, or it may have lost its fullness and been pulled virtually flat, but it takes a good deal of experience to recognise the look of an aerodynamically efficient sail.

Angle of attack

It is actually quite easy to find the correct angle of attack. This is the angle at which the apparent wind meets the sail and is measured to the sail's chord. For example the sail should not be sheeted in close on a beam reach because the driving force would be considerably reduced. Full driving force cannot develop because laminar flow to leeward breaks down and does not extend the full width of the sail. Air flow breaks away and becomes turbulent which hinders the establishment of low pressure to leeward and, consequently, the vital difference in pressure. In practice the boardsailor should sheet his sail in to the point where it just stops lifting and no further.

Steering a sailboard

Landlubbers, and even those sailors who know nothing about boardsailing, are always asking how the board is steered. They often watch uncomprehendingly as a boardsailor returns to the beach, making his way between swimmers so accurately that there seems to be no chance of an accident. How can the board be steered when it has no rudder?

The sum of all the forces produced by a sail can be imagined as acting through a single point which is called the centre of effect (CE) of the sail and is crucial when boardsailing. It is not identical with the geometric centre of the sail area which does not alter and can easily be found by drawing lines from the corners of the sail to bisect the opposite sides. The centre of the sail is where the lines cross. But wind pressure on the sail acts on a curved surface and the position of the CE therefore depends both on the angle of attack and on the wind speed. In practice the CE lies above the geometric centre of the sail and moves nearer to or further from

Left: The angle of attack. The sail should be trimmed so that its chord is no closer than 15°–20° to the apparent wind.

Right: The sail has been sheeted in far too much and causes the air flow to break away to leeward into turbulence. Instead of pressure being low to leeward the turbulence mainly has a braking effect.

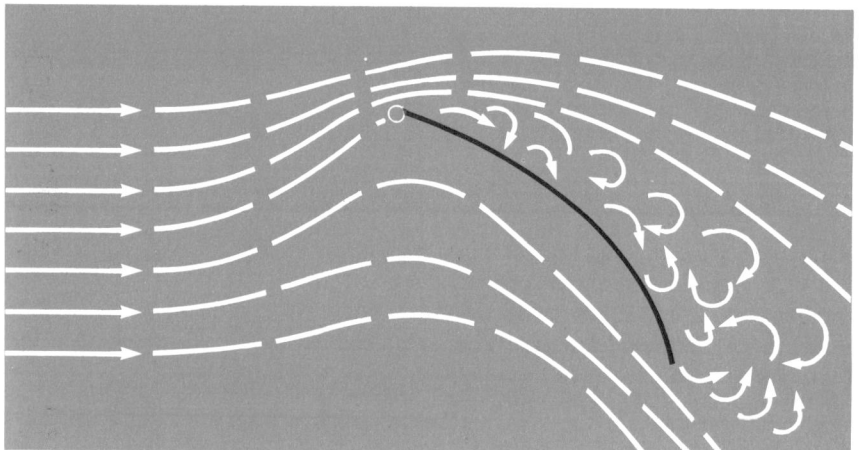

the luff depending on sail camber and wind speed.

Beneath the water the daggerboard, fin and the submerged part of the hull together make up the total lateral area which counters the leeway component of the sail force and which therefore discourages the board from slipping to leeward. The forces act through a point which is called the centre of lateral resistance (CLR) which is similarly not identical to the geometric centre of this lateral area.

To achieve directional balance the total driving force (CE) must act through the same vertical plane, and in an opposite direction, to the CLR. However, finding the exact position of the CE depends on careful measurement of many factors such as, angle of heel of rig, position of camber of the sail, angle of attack of the sail and the sheeting angle. The result is of practical interest to the sailor but totally impractical to find. Just remember that to achieve equilibrium the centre of effort has to lie more or less ahead of the centre of lateral resistance *when viewed from the side*. The board will then sail a straight course because sail and lateral area are balanced.

The basic difference between a sailing boat and a sailboard now

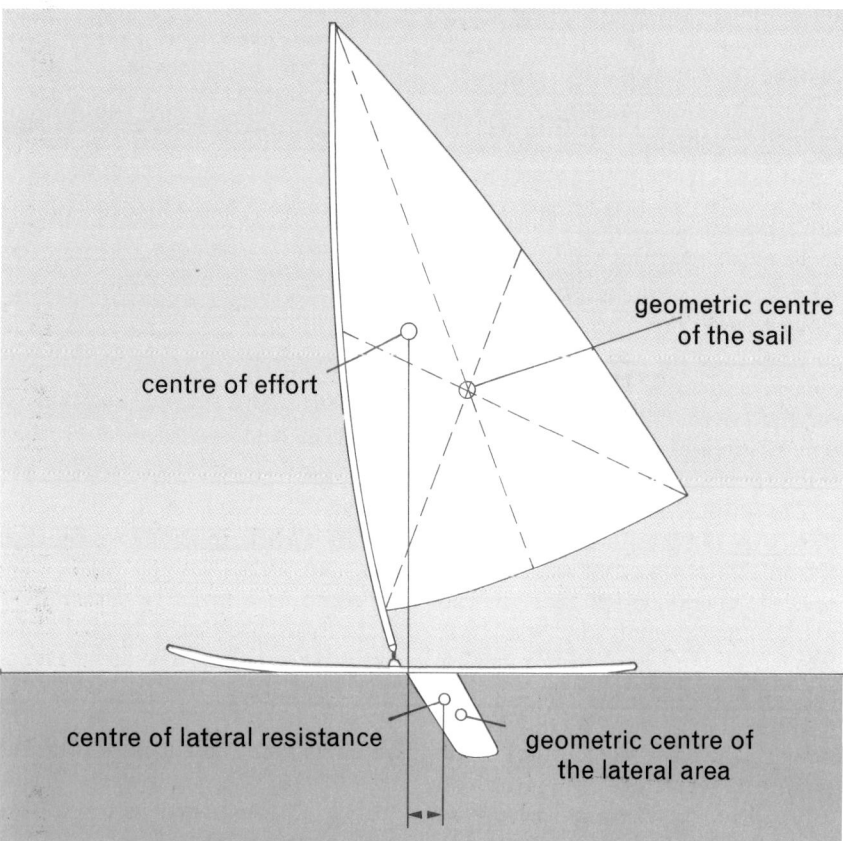

The centre of effort is impossible to place with accuracy and, in any case, varies a little with speed. If it lies just forward of the centre of lateral resistance, when viewed from the side, the board will be directionally balanced and will sail straight.

When the boardsailor rakes the mast forward the centre of effort moves well forward of the centre of lateral resistance. This forces the bow to leeward, pivoting round the centre of lateral resistance. The sailboard bears away.

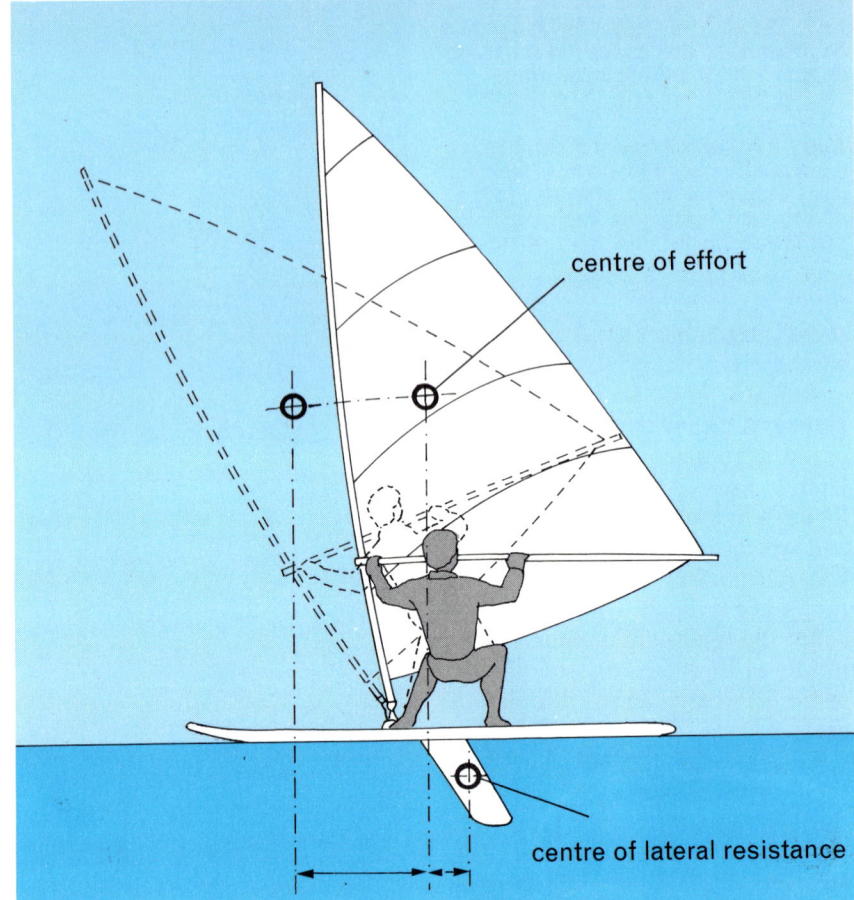

becomes clear. A boat has a fixed mast and therefore requires a rudder to alter course and override misbalance. A sailboard on the other hand has a mast which can be moved in any direction to adjust balance and therefore needs no rudder. To bear away the rig merely has to be raked forward, so shifting the CE forward of the CLR. On the other hand when the boardsailor rakes the rig further aft the CE moves aft of the CLR and the board luffs up.

And that is the whole secret as to why a sailboard can be steered although it has no rudder.

A few points to complete the picture. Because the sailboard has no rudder there is no braking effect due to resistance, an effect that is particularly noticeable when a rudder is put hard over. This is another reason why a sailboard is one of the fastest of sailing craft.

The principle of altering course purely by shifting the position of the CE in relation to that of the CLR must be understood so that you can work out automatically what will happen as a result of using a smaller sail or a special daggerboard. For example if you use a pivoting centreboard the CLR will shift aft at the same instance that you raise it, say on a broad reach. Therefore when you raise the board you simultaneously have to rake the mast slightly further aft to bring the CE back above the CLR again and so keep on a straight course.

This is a help in strong winds when you can either use a small daggerboard or a pivoting centreboard in the raised position instead of a full-sized daggerboard. The advantage is that the mast doest not then need to be raked quite so far forward and, as the boom will also be slightly lower, the rig can be supported more easily. Above all the board will not have such a strong inclination to luff up and this makes it much easier to get under way.

Altering the area of the sail has a similar effect. If you take the same daggerboard but use the all-round sail which is one square metre (ten square feet) smaller you have to change your sailing technique. The CE will be as high as with the normal sail and, consequently, when a gust eases the area of the sail is high enough and catches enough wind for you to be able to pull yourself back onto the board. But the most important point is that the CE of the all-round sail lies further forward, because the area has been reduced only at the leech, and this has the same effect on balance as using a raised centreboard. The board loses its tendency to luff up sharply in fresh winds, so making it easier for you to start when the wind is strong and to sail through heavy gusts (cf p. 121). Also the area is smaller.

So you can use your knowledge to choose an appropriate daggerboard or sail and, in this way, adapt your board and rig to match your requirements and technique in strong winds, surf, gusty weather and high seas.

Adjustment of sail camber

A boardsailor can tune his wind engine to deliver maximum power in just the same way as a driving enthusiast can tune his car engine. The important difference between the two is of course the simplicity of a sailboard by comparison with a highly developed and complicated technical product such as a racing engine. The adjustments for sail camber, and hence power output, are simply the luff downhaul and the clew outhaul. The height of the boom on the mast has only a limited effect.

But let us be absolutely clear that, when it comes to speed, correct technique plus the ability to gybe and tack quickly are far more important than just tuning the sail to perfection. With normal sailing boats the tuning is more of a race winning factor but with boardsailing the technique is decisive. So, bearing this in mind, these are the basic facts about sail tuning.

The stability of cut and shape of a

How to adjust sail camber. Pull downhaul and outhaul taut to flatten the sail for strong winds (left).

Slacken downhaul and outhaul to make the sail fuller for light breezes (right).

The difference between sailboards and sailing boats is that although the sailors in each case lean out to windward when the wind is strong, the sailing boat heels to leeward (left) whereas the sailboard's mast is tilted to windward (right).

sailboard's sail depends entirely on the quality of the cloth which should stretch as little as possible or, at least, in a way that can be controlled by the sailmaker. You cannot easily check this when buying the sail except that you cannot correct a poorly cut sail by adjusting its camber.

It is the flexibility of the mast and the curve that is cut on the sail luff that enables a full sail to be flattened so easily. All GRP masts are extraordinarily flexible while aluminium masts are usually stiffer. To flatten a sail set on a flexible mast just increase the tension on the downhaul and the clew outhaul. The mast then curves forward and pulls flat the fullness that is provided by the luff curve.

You can try this out very quickly for yourself. If you just tauten the downhaul and leave the outhaul quite slack the mast will bend slightly. If you then tension the outhaul to the maximum the pull acts directly on the mast and bends it more. When outhaul and downhaul are both tensioned the curvature of the sail is very much reduced and the point of maximum camber is also shifted further forward. As it moves forward the leech slackens in the upper part of the sail and allows the air to exhaust more easily. This reduces the leeward force on the sail and makes it much easier to support the rig in a fresh breeze. Always use both downhaul and outhaul together to adjust fullness. The rules for sail tuning are:

- A full sail when the wind is light.
- The harder the wind, the flatter the sail.

The reason for adjusting the camber of a sailboard's sail is rather different from that for a conventional boat with a fixed mast. A boat uses a flatter sail in strong winds to control excessive heeling which the crew are unable to counter by shifting their weight outboard.

A sailboard, on the other hand, does not heel because the universal joint allows the mast to incline in any direction. In fresh breezes the boardsailor actually pulls the rig over to windward and, provided he is fit enough and sufficiently skilful, he can convert into board speed all the tremendous drive delivered by a full sail in strong winds. Nor does he have to concern himself with increased leeway force thrusting rig and board to leeward because the tilted rig actually gives lift which aids speed. So, you can see that first class technique is much more important than tuning the sail perfectly.

The height of the boom on the mast does not affect the shape of the sail greatly and, in any case, the gap in the sleeve where the boom is attached leaves little room for adjustment. When the boom is made fast lower down mast bend is affected and the direction in which the outhaul pulls at the after end of the boom is altered. Both affect the shape of the sail but only to a small extent. It is far more important to find the height where the boardsailor can grasp the boom most comfortably and this will depend entirely on his height, the length of his arms and his personal technique. You can only find the right height by trial and error and by sailing a great deal.

The weather

The weather is a never-ending subject for those who sail in boats but the boardsailor's interest is generally confined to whether it will be baking hot or whether rain is forecast yet again for the following weekend! Too strong a wind or too little will affect his sport but medium term and long term forecasts matter little because, unlike many other water users, the boardsailor generally stays very close to the shore. He is seldom out for more than an hour or two.

Furthermore should he get caught out he can abandon sailing for a short time, even in the worst of weather, and this is something a conventional boat sailor cannot do. The boardsailor just lowers his rig onto the water, and sits on his board. He can do this between two races, when visibility is bad, in heavy gusts, high seas or a thunderstorm—most of which are conditions that need the maximum of concentration if a normal sailor is to avoid capsizing.

The way that weather develops can be complicated and obscure, but the boardsailor needs to understand two points:

- The characteristics of land and sea breezes (temporary offshore and onshore winds).
- The sequence of events during a thunderstorm.

Highs, lows and wind

Global weather results from the combined effects of atmospheric pressure, temperature and humidity, and variations caused by the sun's heat. However the boardsailor is concerned only with the short term effects and variations between night and day and not so much with the effects of the seasons or the earth's rotation.

Wind is a movement of air which results from two completely different but interacting factors. The first is differences in atmospheric pressure which are common to adjacent areas everywhere to a greater or lesser degree. The second more local effect is due to the heating of land and water by the rays of the sun.

An anticyclone, or *high*, is an area where atmospheric pressure is high.

Left: Boardsailors relaxing between races. It is easy to sit and rest like this, stopping to enjoy a chat or eat a second breakfast, even in the heaviest of weather.

Above: Capsized. This cannot happen to boardsailors. A dinghy sailor who loses control for a second in a strong wind will easily end up in the water because his racing boat reacts extremely sensitively. Righting a capsized dinghy can be hard work.

The High over central Europe has a central pressure of 1020 millibars while the central pressure of the Low over the northern North Sea is 1000 mb. The difference between these pressures results in a force 6 wind in the southern North Sea.

A depression, or *low*, is the opposite and is usually associated with stronger winds and moist air revolving round in a spiral.

Lows move quite rapidly and range from very local thundery centres to huge areas covering a large part of the North Atlantic for example. Winds are relatively strong, especially near the centre of the spiral, with rain and poor visibility until the centre has passed, after which there is a clearance, the temperature drops and winds become gusty.

Highs do not usually move much and are associated with lighter winds and settled weather, but can often bring misty conditions for long periods.

Wind tends to blow from higher towards lower pressure areas, but do not do so directly owing to the earth's rotational effects. Wind blows spirally in towards the centre of a Low, counter-clockwise in the northern hemisphere, clockwise in the south of the globe. It also blows spirally out from a High, clockwise in the north and counter-clockwise in the southern hemispheres.

The greater differences in pressure, the stronger will be the winds. For example a pressure difference across the North Sea of 20 millibars would cause a wind of Force 6 (say 25 knots).

- *pressure differences* govern general weather conditions.
- *temperature differences* caused by the sun's heat locally, have a big effect on local weather.

The symbol means 'Southerly, wind force 6'
H = High pressure area; T = Low pressure area.

Land and sea breezes

The effect of the sun each day on land and water breeds a completely different wind system. These are local winds which are of short duration and are caused because land is heated much more rapidly than water by the sun's rays, and cools more quickly.

In the early morning it takes a little while for heat from the sun to take effect but soon the warm air over the land, which is heated more quickly, starts to rise and a small low pressure area is formed towards which flows air from over the cooler water. This is the sea breeze which always blows towards the shore. When the general weather situation is relatively stable you can expect a sea breeze to start between about 10 and midday on sunny days. Its maximum strength could reach about force 5 in the early afternoon, and that is the best time for sailors and boardsailors. The sea breeze drops at sunset and you can often see the area of smooth water

The sun is setting. The fresh breeze that has been blowing during the day is easing and will soon drop completely. The boardsailor should make his way home in good time.

The sea breeze is drawn in from the water to replace the rising air above the sun-warmed land (top).

At night the land breeze is drawn towards the sea because the land cools more quickly than the water (bottom).

A strong onshore breeze is fine for boardsailing because it is so steady. Be careful if the shore is stony or if there are cliffs along the coast (right).

spreading gradually offshore in the evening. In rivers and fjords the wind first drops right inland because the air is cooled more quickly there, but there will still be a good sailing breeze offshore.

The process is reversed at night. Unlike the water, land cools very quickly at sunset. Air rises above the now warmer water and the local low pressure area formed draws in cooled air from the land. The nightly land breeze starts to blow, offshore, but just as reliably as the sea breeze.

These winds occur relatively constantly all along the coasts, but inland waters have to be of a certain size to generate a worthwhile wind. When they do occur they are usually much stronger than those found on the coast. Woods, open heathland and varying heights of land nearby impede or accentuate the thermal effect. In particular the friction arising from the rough surface of the land afffects the wind. There is little frictional resistance from the open sea, even when waves are high, and the wind stays relatively steady, but inland the surface is rarely level. Low hills, a range of moderately high mountains or irregularly built-over suburbs may extend for miles from the shore. Friction basically reduces the speed of the wind, but the wind also becomes gusty.

In the foothills of high mountains, such as the Alps, strong downdraughts often surprise the sailor. They are caused by the great differences in temperature of sunny and shaded slopes. The character and development of weather are therefore much affected by local peculiarities. The wind is funnelled between mountain chains, in valleys and on long narrow lakes, the latter being a boardsailor's delight. This combination of thermal effects and funnelling is the inland sailor's compensation for the plentiful supply of wind in coastal waters and many larger lakes are a paradise for boardsailors because the wind is so reliable.

The Alps and other mountainous areas present a major obstacle to weather development. Local and very marked winds are found within the framework of the regular and generally repetitive pattern of highs and lows. These winds have to be respected being often sudden and violent. Notorious and best-known in Europe are the *föhn*, a warm wind which bursts over the Alpine barriers and the *mistral* which funnels down the Rhône valley to the sea. Both of these are much appreciated by boardsailors in the area even though they often blow at gale force.

Even an advanced boardsailor should have great respect for these sudden winds and seek the safety of the shore in good time. The abruptness with which they strike is always surprising and they are particularly dangerous to a boardsailor if, for example, he has set off from a narrow sandy beach in a long cliffy coast, or if an offshore wind threatens to drive him away from the land. The consequences of getting caught could be catastrophic in either case.

For his own safety the boardsailor must find out local wind conditions when he is sailing in an area he does not know. The best advice will be obtained from inhabitants such as fishermen, sailors and, of course, local boardsailors. Storm warning systems operate on many lakes and sometimes there are acoustic as well as visual signals. In some areas it is a legal requirement to return immediately to the nearest bank when an urgent storm warning has been given.

Quite apart from official warnings you must always keep an eye on the development of the weather, especially inland where the situation can change with great speed. Deterioration can almost always be anticipated by studying cloud formation so check frequently all round the horizon but especially to the west where most weather originates in both hemispheres.

Thunderstorms

A real thunderstorm with wind! An unsuspecting boardsailor, frustrated by lack of wind, can yearn for this on a heavy sweltering airless day. Unsuspecting? Do not yearn for danger! Learn to survive however, if you get into unexpected trouble.

A boardsailor caught in a thunderstorm out of the water has to face two dangers, that of being driven downwind when he can no longer sail against the squalls and the much smaller risk of being struck by lightning.

A thunderstorm develops when high temperatures coincide with a very humid atmosphere. Heat causes air to rise very rapidly and it can shoot up to a height of 10 km (6 miles). There it cools and the moisture condenses into drops of water or ice which are too heavy to be supported by the rising air and fall as thundery rail or hail. All this is accompanied by violent gusts. The static electricity generated as moisture condenses is discharged as lightning which travels between clouds or down to earth when the charge becomes excessive.

One cannot fail to spot the formation of a thunderstorm with its dark tower of clouds reaching skyward. When thick cumulus clouds concentrate at one point on the horizon and start to soar upwards, with an anvil-shaped cap spreading sideways, you know there will be a thunderstorm soon.

Thundery areas can persist for some days with local storms popping up here and there. A big disturbance can completely knock out the prevailing pressure-generated wind over a wide area. A feature then is flat calms, alternating with winds from any direction, plus violent brief storms which seldom last more than an hour or two.

There is only one thing for the boardsailor to do when caught out and that is to get back to the shore in good time. If this is impossible keep your head, lower the rig onto the water and crouch on the board with your feet together. This is also the safest position to avoid the unlikely event of being struck by lightning. Remember—it won't last long.

Below: This is how a thunderstorm develops.

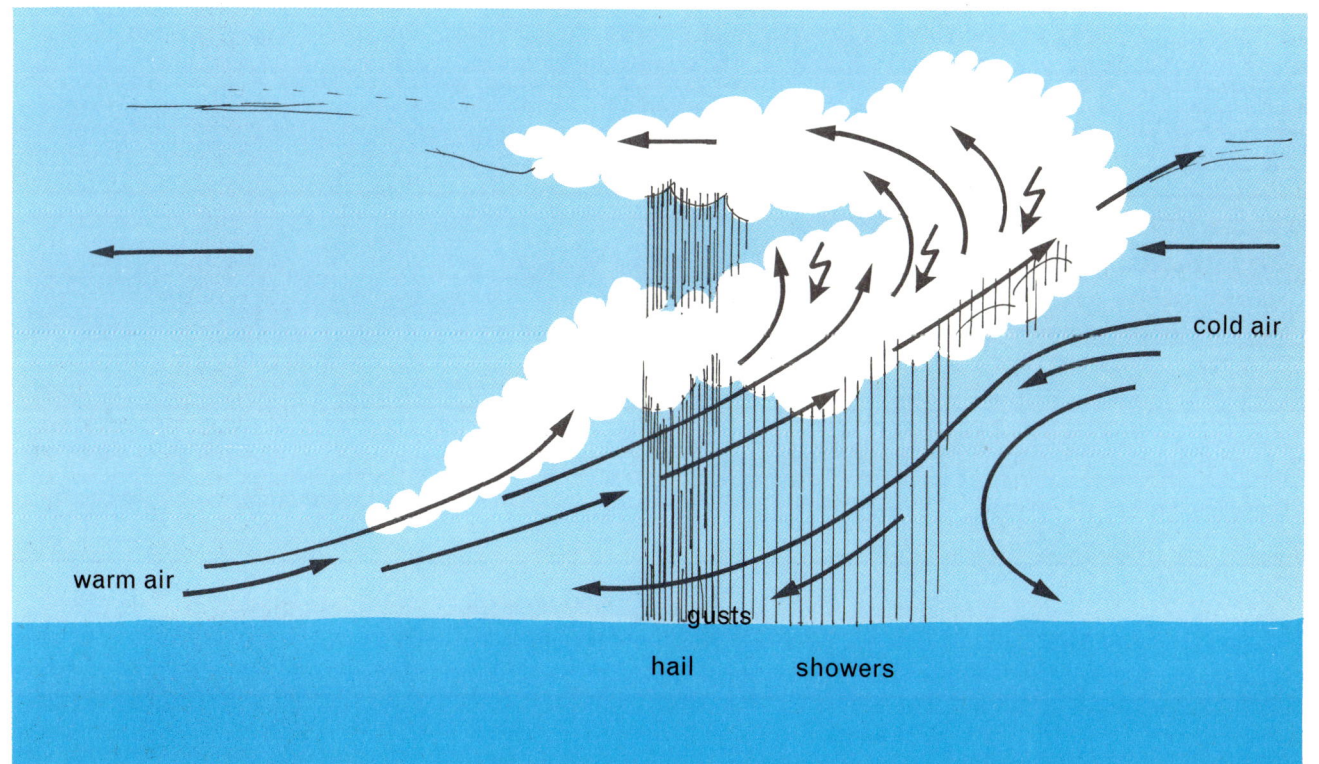

Safety

Not long ago boardsailing was considered a dangerous sport. People were always falling in and could not steer properly. Dangerous also meant dangerous to other people and so the authorities were quick to step in with prohibitions and set aside specific areas for boardsailing. Although a yachtsman still sometimes feels he must 'rescue' a boardsailor thinking he has capsized, when he is only sitting comfortably on his board with his rig on the water, the sailboard has now become recognised as a proper sailing craft. Its characteristics not only make it more manoeuvrable than other craft but also impose limitations. A boardsailor cannot exhibit a fixed light on the mast, carry a lamp in his hand or fit a compass to his board; things that in some countries are enforced legally, at night and in fog. The boardsailor is so close to the water that he must be able to see around, and be seen, all the time, and this is impossible when it is dark. Fog rarely forms suddenly so the boardsailor should make his way back to the shore at the first sign of fog and before he loses his sense of direction.

Safety measures are important because it is only by avoiding accidents that prohibitions or restrictions for boardsailors can be avoided!

No sailboards should be out at night or in fog.

The boardsailor's safety rules

1. *A wet suit is essential.* Cold caused by condensation is the boardsailor's greates enemy and he is helpless when suffering from hypothermia. Even at the height of summer, the longer you intend to sail the more important it is to wear at least a 'shortie', particularly for the protection of the kidneys.

2. *Inspect your gear* for damage before starting out. Replace chafed control lines and mend small tears in the sail with adhesive tape.

3. *Attach the rig to the board* with a safety line. They will then at least stay connected if the mast foot releases. If they do become separated go after the board first. It drifts more quickly.

4. *Take a spare line* with you. Lash it securely to the forward part of the boom where it is easiest to get at.

5. *Get some local knowledge.* Is there a special local wind, underwater rocks etc?

6. *Study the conditions.* Watch out for offshore winds, currents and tidal streams. If you cannot sail to windward well, stay close to the shore.

7. *Avoid bathing beaches.* Do not endanger swimmers unnecessarily. Often only a head is visible above the water.

8. *Learn the right-of-way rule* (see page 96) and comply with them.

9. *Avoid shipping channels.* Do not hinder professional seamen unnecessarily. Alter course in plenty of time. In light winds it takes longer to give way and this can lead to danger.

10. *In an emergency* never leave your board under any circumstances. It is a safe life-float and can be paddled much faster than you can swim. Learn the internationally recognised distress signal.

The international distress signal. Keep raising your arms above your head and lowering them again.

Right-of-way rules

Sailboards have to share the water with many other vessels, perhaps pleasure craft of all types, under sail and power, as well as small fishing boats, ferries and excursion steamers, while large freighters and liners may pass not far away. These all need space in which to sail and manoeuvre and traffic regulations are therefore required, just as on the roads, if collisions are to be avoided.

The international Regulations for Preventing Collisions at Sea, and the inland waterways rules valid in various countries, are based on the fact that large ships manoeuvre relatively slowly, cover a long distance before stopping and draw a lot of water, quite apart from economics which require commercial shipping to be able to proceed at night and, to some extent, even in fog.

Long distance boardsailing rules

If not attended by a motor boat always stay close to the bank or coast. Do not cruise alone. An observer on land may be enough, but this depends on the weather and the area. Safest is to be accompanied by a motor boat with at least two crew, one to control the boat and one to give help. Take spares such as sail, battens, mast.

Carry distress signals (mini flares), a small first aid kit, storm sail and perhaps something to drink and some chocolate in a rucksack or bum-bag.

Give notice of your intended destination and approximate time of arrival.

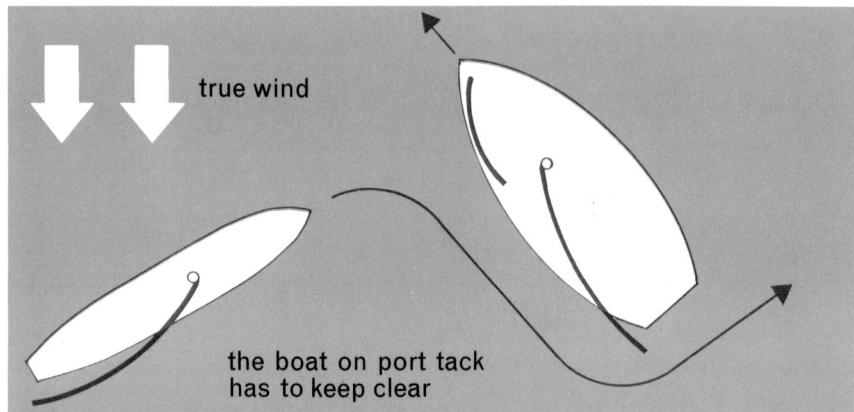

Giving way when sailing on opposite tacks.

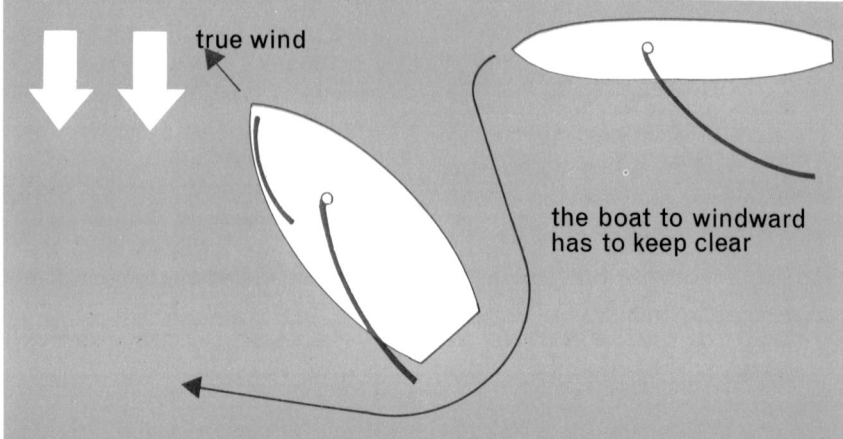

Giving way when sailing on the same tack.

> **Basic right-of-way rule**
> All vessels must be conducted in such a way that traffic can proceed safely and easily. No vessel may endanger, damage or, except in unavoidable circumstances, inconvenience or obstruct another vessel. All the precautionary measures appropriate to the prevailing circumstances and conditions must be taken, with due regard to the observation of good seamanship.

■ Many of the rules do not apply to sailboards, for example because they do not sail at night or in fog. Furthermore a sailboard is quite extraordinarily maneouvrable and can alter course instantly, give way and stop. It draws very little, cannot anchor, does not use a harbour, need not worry about shoals or sandbanks, and can therefore avoid any obstruction, however unexpected.

Sailboards are classed as sailing boats in the right of way rules because they use the same motive power, the wind. The three basic right of way rules for sailing vessels are:

1. When sailing on opposite tacks: a boat on port tack with the wind on the port side keeps clear of a boat on starboard tack.
2. When sailing on the same tack: a boat to windward keeps out of the way of a boat to leeward.
3. When overtaking: an overtaking boat keeps out of the way of the boat being overtaken.

To help you remember, wrap coloured adhesive tape round the boom between the places where your mast and sheet hand grip it, using green (the starboard colour) on the starboard side and red (the port colour) on the port side. When your course crosses that of another sailboard or sailing boat on the opposite tack just glance down between your hands.

Green = go—you have right of way
Red = danger—you must keep out of the way

The rules for same tacks (windward keeps clear) and overtaking (overtaker keeps clear) are easy to remember.

Keep a good look-out all around you. As well as altering course in good time, do so postively so that other craft can see that you are giving way. Always insist on your rights: but make sure the board or boat which has to give way has seen you by hailing in good time. Be prepared, however, for last minute avoidance if things go wrong.

Personal buoyancy aids

The buoyancy provided by wet suits is not adequate to keep a boardsailor afloat and a buoyancy aid or life jacket is advisable, especially when learning in colder waters where there is an increased danger of hypothermia and when sailing in rough seas or surf. Some regatta rules call for all sailors to wear at least minimum amount of extra buoyancy.

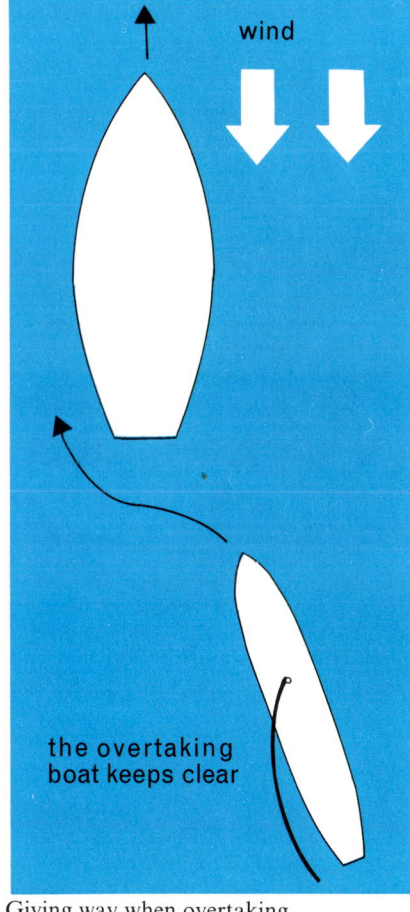

Giving way when overtaking.

Restrictions

Although local authorities watched with mistrust in the early years of boardsailing, restrictions have generally been reasonable. In areas where shipping is heavy the aim is that shipping should not endanger sailboards while boardsailors should not hamper shipping. In some places, boardsailing is prohibited at night, in shipping channels and within 200 m of harbour entrances, anchorages and moorings.

Up to now complete prohibition of boardsailing in particular inland waters is the exception—fortunately. It is good sense to ban boardsailing in areas marked out for water skiing, for example, boardsailors are sometimes restricted to water 100 metres from the shore, and lanes have to be used to sail out there. In countries where the sailboard boom is less intense the restrictions are fewer but may increase.

So if you intend to sail in a new area do not just enquire about local peculiarities near the shore and wind conditions but check whether there are any local bye-laws.

Fun, fabulous and free! This is boardsailing!

Ulrich Stanciu

Part 2 ADVANCED BOARDSAILING

Basic technique in strong winds

It is enough to drive you to despair. You have learnt how to handle your board well, you can balance easily, know how to tack and gybe and can sail in all directions without getting tired—always providing the wind is no stronger than force 3. But suddenly you meet stronger winds and everything changes. You keep falling in without knowing why, the board is out of control, and so is the sail. You realise that, obviously, your technique is inadequate. But take heart, this experience is shared by all boardsailors, and we can put it right.

The first time that you take your board with your for a seaside holiday you see that the wave crests trail white foam and gusts whip up the water. Somewhere in this welter of foam you clamber onto the board, heave yourself to your feet and struggle to pull up the sail, only to find yourself hurled into the water the moment you try to get under way. After twenty or thirty abortive attempts you are washed up on the beach, murderously angry and more than tempted to sell the board and give up the sport.

But wait, do not give up, you are really not far from becoming an expert strong-wind boardsailor! Just look at the fascinating photographs and see how effortlessly these experenced boardsailors master a strong wind. How on earth do they do it? They must all be acrobats and incredibly strong! Strength plays a part of course, but the right technique is far more important than sheer muscle. Living proof of this is the 1977 Windsurfer World champion who was 15 years old. In spite of strength-sapping force 5–6 winds little Robby Naish sailed right away from his older, and certainly stronger opponents in a marathon race in Sardinia. Back on the beach everybody was debating how this youngster could cope with such a strong wind, and the answer was that his technique was right.

Even without the extra thrill of planing over the water on a sailboard, strong winds are an exciting challenge. Correct technique is more important than strength.

The force 4 hurdle

In force 3 winds the wind pressure on a normal-sized sail is about 17 kg or 37½ lbs. The boardsailor counters this pressure by using the weight of his body, converting it through the board into forward speed. A force 4 wind, only one force higher, exerts double the pressure on the sail and 34 kg or 75 lbs is a force that will easily pull a man standing upright off his feet unless he leans far back to counter the pressure.

This doubling of wind pressure on the sail is the reason for the difficulties that arise at force 4. Instead of the wind being a gentle force driving the board forward it suddenly seems to rush at the sail like a wild bull that has to be parried.

Here are some hints which will help you get over the force 4 hurdle so that you can learn quickly how to sail in force 4–5 and, using a storm sail, in even stronger winds. The small but vital difference is:

. . . mast to windward

Before attempting to put strong wind boardsailing into practice we must first revert to theory so that you are absolutely clear as to the basic difference between sailing and boardsailing. A sailing boat heels to leeward as the wind freshens, that is, the sail is forced away in the direction to

In stronger winds you not only pull on the boom with your arms, but have to use all your weight and lean back towards the wind.

The difference between a surfboard and an ordinary boat. The wind force is balanced by leaning the rig towards the wind (left) and by allowing the rig to lean away and spill wind (right).

which the wind blows. The harder the wind blows the more the boat heels and, because then the projected area of sail is smaller, the pressure of the wind is reduced. A sailing boat therefore remains in a state of equilibrium with wind pressure balanced by the weight of the crew and/or ballast keel.

To obtain the same effect when boardsailing, namely to reduce the sail area and to balance wind pressure with body weight, the sail has to be pulled over to windward, that is, beyond the vertical and towards the wind. The boardsailor leans the weight of his body backwards to counter the wind pressure and this simultaneously reduces the projected sail area. Both combine to balance the increased strength of the wind and the sailboard will then be in a state of equilibrium.

To start with it is difficult to get used to leaning back against the wind because the position seems so unnatural. Up till now you have been accustomed to just standing on the board and, instinctively, you feel that if you lean back you will fall in. But

In a real blow, keep your arms straight but relaxed. This avoids wasting extra energy when using the weight of your body to hang out under the rig.

for strong wind boardsailing it is absolutely essential to abandon this upright stance and to learn a new technique. It is impossible to counter the wind pressure on the sail without using the whole weight of your body.

But how do you get into this fascinating position, planing close above the surface of the water with the sail pulled far over to windward? Here is a list of the main difficulties you will meet when getting under way and sailing in strong winds, and we will then work through them in detail.

- It is not easy to pull the sail out of the water.
- It is very much more difficult to balance because more wind means larger waves.
- It is harder to co-ordinate movements because you need to concentrate more on balance and on correct sail trim.
- When the board starts to move it tries hard to luff up and turn head to wind.
- When sheeting in the sail the wind pressure is often so great that you cannot hold onto the rig.
- Once under way it is difficult to keep a balance between wind pressure, body weight and wave motion.

And now some advice to help you overcome these difficulties.

Raising the sail

The first stage is no different from before. The board lies across the wind with the sail to leeward on the water, and you climb onto the board from windward, standing centrally with one foot just forward of the mast foot and the other on the daggerboard trunk. Do not catch hold of the uphaul and start heaving immediately because, as soon as the top comes clear of the water, the wind has a surface on which it can act and promptly forces the sail down again. What is more you normally find that a lot of water has collected in the mast sleeve and this makes the rig extra heavy.

Grasp one of the higher knots on the uphaul and start to pull the rig up, in a direction at a slight angle towards the bow so that the water can drain off the leech. Then swing the mast back to the centre of the board with an S-shaped movement which will dip the end of the boom straight down into the water. The sail will

It is hard work getting the sail up in a fresh wind! Bend your hips and knees and help your arms to pull by straightening your legs. The duck, by the way, is not a good idea as a life-jacket!

then be pointing roughly towards the wind and thus gives minimum resistance.

Now pull hard on the uphaul, moving from knot to knot until the end of the boom is clear of the water. It is very important that the boom clears the water as soon as possible to allow the sail to shake freely. It is a help if you bend your knees before raising the sail and straighten them as you haul up the rig. Your thighs will then do most of the work and legs are stronger than arms.

If the sail is lying to windward instead of to leeward there are two ways of getting it back to the right side. You can pull the uphaul to bring the top of the sail out of the water and the wind will then get beneath it and whip the rig over to the other side. You need to be rather skilful to do this because you have to turn round like lightning as the sail slams over. The other less risky but more tedious method of shifting the sail from windward to leeward is to pull on the uphaul slightly so that just the very tip of the sail emerges from the water. The wind pushes this either to port or starboard and you can turn the whole board about its own axis. As the board approaches the point where the sail lies directly to leeward you start to pull on the uphaul to raise the sail. You use more strength for this method, but it is considerably more certain.

If you should fall into the water in the process try to turn the board far enough while you are falling for the sail to lie to leeward and you will then avoid having to repeat this laborious procedure. With a little practice you will find that you soon become adept.

Balance

When you have raised the sail stand in the mast abeam position ready to get underway. Stay in this position for some time and concentrate entirely on the motion of the waves. There is no short cut to getting your balance on the board. You just have to get used to the see-saw motion and learn to react to it automatically. Your feet will be in the centre of the board of course because the centre of gravity of your body must be amidships.

Keep your ankle, knee and hip joints relaxed and ready to respond to the movement of the waves. Give yourself plenty of time to get used to the motion, waiting until you no longer find it difficult to balance on the board. Only then will you be able to get the knack of getting under way and avoid another swim.

Another point: so far you have held the rig nearly upright but if you stretch your arms a little and let it tilt slightly away from you towards the water you will find that you can lean slightly backwards against its weight and this is less effort. When you pull it back towards you again you have to return your body virtually upright again.

Co-ordination of movement

When you have become accustomed to the motion of the waves, reacting to it almost automatically, do not attempt to get under way immediately but think through the sequence of movements that lead up to starting. Don't grab the boom and sheet it in straight away to get sailing. The more quietly and rationally you proceed the better your chances of a successful take-off in strong wind.

It is definitely an advantage to practise on dry land before making an attempt on the water, and you do not even need a simulator for this, just your own rig. Find a place where the wind is blowing steadily at force 4 or 5, stand with one foot on the mast foot and raise the rig. Just as when you are on the water. Now follow through the procedure you have already learnt for getting under way. You will find that the wind pressure on the sail keeps trying to tear you off your feet to leeward. Hang right back against it and try to counter this pressure with your strength and body weight until you find a stable position which you can hold.

Once you have succeeded in pulling the mast over to windward and in hanging beneath the boom on dry land you will find it much easier to get under way on the water in strong winds. The great advantage of practising like this is that you don't fall in!

1. Support the rig in the same way as you learnt during instruction.

2. Now the mast hand grips the wishbone while the sail shakes in the wind.

5. The harder the wind blows the further you should pull the mast to windward. This turns your body towards the direction in which you will be sailing.

6. Your sheet hand grasps the wishbone and sheets in gradually while you lean your body back against the wind.

3. The sheet hand drops the uphaul and you have time to balance the rig and prepare to start.

4. Important: in strong winds pull the sail over to windward.

7. The pressure of the wind on the sail is balanced by your weight.

8. Practise hanging out like this on the beach in a strong wind until you find your balance.

9. It does not matter if you sit down—just start again.

Ready for take-off

Now back to the water. You will have taken a big step towards getting the feel of starting in strong winds by practising on land and, a very important point, you will not have tired yourself out. On the water, too, try to use skill rather than brute force. You will probably find that the board has turned a little while you were raising the sail and is no longer at the essential 90° to the wind (mast abeam position). So incline the mast towards the bow or stern using the uphaul, and the board will immediately swing back to the exact cross-wind position by slightly raking the mast back and forth.

And now, let's go! Place your front foot just aft of the mast foot, your back foot just aft of the daggerboard case and hold the uphaul close under the boom with both hands. Your mast hand drops the uphaul and passes over the sheet hand to grasp the boom about 20 cm (8 ins) aft of the mast. The sail continues to shake in the wind. Release the uphaul entirely and, for a few seconds, use your sheet hand just to help you keep your balance. With your mast hand pull the boom towards you, then push it away again, and repeat this until you can do it without losing your balance because, at this stage, you will be very wobbly. The sail must be absolutely free to shake in the wind all the time.

To start use the normal procedure but rake the mast so far to windward that the end of the boom points up at an angle before sheeting in the sail.

Why? There are two reasons. First, you have learnt already that a sailboard is steered by shifting the centre of effort in relation to the centre of lateral resistance, and that a board sails straight ahead when the centre of effort (CE) is directly above the centre of lateral resistance (CLR). These normally coincide when the boom is parallel to the water. If you were to sheet in the sail before the boom was parallel to the water, or pointing upward slightly, the board would luff up and probably throw you off.

The second reason is that, when the wind is strong, you have to make full use of your weight and this you can only do if you tilt the mast so far to windward that you can hang beneath the sail. So, before starting to sheet in the sail you tilt the mast

well over to windward and then, as you sheet in, the mast will automatically turn and be raked forward which will cause the board to bear away slightly when it gets under way. The rig is still raked well to windward after the sail has been sheeted in and, because the projected sail area is smaller, the wind pressure on it is reduced and you can counter this with the weight of your body.

The most important rule when getting under way in a strong wind is therefore:

- The stronger the wind the further must the mast be raked to windward before attempting to get under way.

When you tilt the rig so far to windward with your mast hand you will automatically turn your body slightly towards the direction in which you will be moving. Pause in this position for a second or two and check whether the board has luffed up a little in the meanwhile. If it has, just push the rig slightly towards the bow to turn the board back to mast abeam position. The sail will of course still be shaking freely.

Now grasp the boom with your sail hand about three feet further aft than your mast hand. Do not sheet in too fast because the sudden impact of wind pressure would probably pull you over. Quite apart from that the board accelerates so suddenly that you could lose your balance.

The board shoots over the water and the rig is raked well to windward. The boardsailor thrusts the board forward in the direction of motion with his front foot.

These two photographs clearly show strong wind boardsailing technique. The body is held not over the board but close above the water. Much of the fascination of boardsailing is because you are so close to the elements.

Sheeting in gradually

Although the wind is strong you need only sheet in the sail gently, without using much strength. The wind will then only fill a small part of the sail and the board will gather way slowly, rather like a car in first gear. Remember to keep the mast raked well to windward. Once the board has started to move forward sheet in slightly more—the board will then move faster—then sheet in further still—and so on.

In this way you slowly get the feel of the wind strength but you use relatively little effort because the further you sheet in the sail the more you lean out against the wind. You are therefore always in a state of equilibrium. Another important point is to bend your back knee gradually as you sheet in. This lowers your centre of gravity until it is close above the board. Your front leg stays almost fully stretched so as to convert the force of the wind into forward motion.

As wind pressure increases stretch your back leg slightly, pushing yourself outboard and to windward. Your body will then be hanging right over the water and, before you have realised it, you will find you are in the very position that, up to now, you have only looked at in photographs with astonishment. The water sprays high and you are planing through it at great speed. You have become a strong wind boardsailor!

Should a gust strike while you are gradually sheeting in the sail just ease out your sheet hand slightly to reduce pressure on the sail, and then start the process of filling the sail gradually again.

Another point: in a strong wind you will feel the effect of the board's frictional resistance as it gathers way, and you have to overcome this by thrusting the board forward with your feet.

You will find it useful later on when racing and surfsailing if you practise standing on the board for as long as possible with the mast raked well to windward and the sail flapping. Grasp the boom with your sail hand and change the direction to

which the board points by gently sheeting the sail in or out or backing it. You will need to be able to do this at the start of a race especially so that you can get your board into the right position as you wait for the starting signal to go. It will also come in useful when surfsailing and waiting for a particular group of waves before getting under way.

To impress all these points on your memory so that they come to mind on the water they are summarised below:

- Use a gentle S-movement when raising the sail, bend your knees slightly before starting to haul and then stretch your legs as you pull.
- Position your feet just aft of the mast foot and aft of the daggerboard trunk.
- Tilt the rig well to windward with your mast hand and check that the board is lying at 90° to the wind.
- Fill the sail with wind in stages and sheet in slowly until you gather way.
- Spill excessive wind immediately by easing out your sheet hand.
- When sheeting in the sail bend your back leg and squat on it, thrusting the board forward with your front foot.

The back leg is well bent and, because this lowers the boardsailor's centre of gravity, the wind has little opportunity to pluck him off the board. Hardly any other sport brings nature so close to your skin.

Boardsailing in a strong wind—speed madness

It happens to everybody. Having got under way for the first time and felt the thrill of sailing ecstatically over the water at full speed, you get really bitten by the boardsailing bug. The sensation of planing through the spray on such a simple apparatus, dependent on yourself alone, leads to an incurable fever.

What is it about strong wind boardsailing that is so exciting? Naturally there is the heightened sensation of speed so close to the water, but this is largely illusory because your board moves barely as fast as a bicycle. The world speed record for a sailboard is 19·1 knots (35·4 km per hour) at present and is held by the Dutchman Derk Thijs. He set it during the John Player Speed Record Week and became the fastest sailor in the 10 square metres maximum sail area class.

Looked at objectively sailboards

Jets of spray mean high speed. The boardsailor feels that he is sailing even faster than he really is because he is too close to the water. The record of 19·1 knots (35·4 km/h) for an ordinary board is faster than all except special record breaking boats can sail.

Boardsailing can be compared to skiing. Skidding over the waves is something like swinging down a steep snow-covered piste. But you learn to boardsail more quickly and it is softer when you fall!

are relatively slow. Some normal ocean ships can move at 27 knots (50 km/h) while high performance catamarans such as the Tornado can also approach this figure. Why then do you have such an impression of speed when boardsailing that you feel as if you are about to fly? Certainly it is partly because your craft is so small and simple, and that you speed close above the surface of the water, literally holding the wind in your hands. Then there is the narrowness of the board, with the water and spray shooting out from the rails even at slower speeds. There is nothing to intervene between you and the elements.

Another attraction of boardsailing in strong winds is the challenge of the waves. You feel a million miles from the normal and protected world. You have only yourself to rely on. You have to decide whether to give up and drift back to shore or to take up the challenge of the mighty wind and waves, pitting your puny strength and intelligence against the power of nature. Techniques improve, and naturally there are any number of dodges which you can use to improve your board-handling in strong winds so that you can sail your board longer in a storm, fall in less often, or make a hair-raising ride on a wave an even longer-lasting thrill.

Finer points of strong wind technique

We have learnt how to get under way quickly and easily. But what happens next? Now you want to sail for as long as you can and safely. A little advice will help.

You are skimming over the water with the mast raked to windward, and are hanging beneath the boom. If you find your forearms are losing strength too quickly you can alter your grip, changing from overhand to underhand. This will ease the load on your sheet hand especially. Try moving your hands back and forth along the boom too to find the position where the pressure of the sail is best distributed between your two hands.

The stronger the wind the further aft should your hands grasp the boom, but the mast hand should never be further than 50 cm (20 ins) from the mast. Above all, when sailing in strong winds make sure that you do not become tense because that will exhaust you very quickly. Try to stay as relaxed as possible while you control the rig with arms outstretched.

Remember the importance of relaxation because one of the most common problems when boardsailing in strong wind is cramp in the forearms caused by the restriction of blood supply. Your forearms take a great deal of strain and, although the heart pumps blood to the muscles, they take time to adjust to the limited amount of oxygen available. The only cure is to lower the sail on the water and sit on the board for a while, raising your arms above your head and massaging them gently. After some minutes you can start sailing again and then, after a while, pause for another 10 minutes, and so on. You will find after one or two days sailing that your forearms have stopped hurting.

This is why a wet suit, cut generously at the elbows and forearms, is the only answer for a strong wind boardsailor. Muscles must not be compressed by excessive taper. Zips along the forearms serve well and can be unzipped quickly when necessary.

Your legs are far less stressed than your arms, but they play a very important part. Before starting you placed your front foot aft of the mast step and, when starting to gather way, you converted the wind pressure on the sail into forward motion by thrusting the board forward with your feet. Now that you are sailing it is still mainly your feet that transmit this pressure, and you can brace your front foot near the mast foot, but be careful not to let your toes get too near the universal joint because they could be pinched in a fall. The front leg, which should be relatively straight, transmits most of the drive while your back leg is used as a flexible lever to move your body outboard and inboard.

Naturally your feet need not always stay in the same place, and once the board has gathered speed you can shift them easily because a board moving at high speed is much more stable than when it is motionless. Experiment to find the most satisfactory positions for your feet, just as you did with your hands on the boom.

If you are to boardsail in strong winds without difficulty it is absolutely essential to have a good foothold. Nothing is more infuriating than to be planing in a superb gust and to slip off the board because the standing surface is too smooth. This has already been mentioned in the beginner's section but, to remind you of the important points:

- Keep sun-tan oil away from the board or clean it thoroughly with a fat-dissolving detergent.
- Wear non-slip shoes. Training shoes with soft flexible rubber soles are fine if they have not become too worn.
- Apply wax to the standing surface. The wax preferred by American surfers is obtainable in most surf-shops and gives a good hold, especially for bare feet. If need be use any method you can devise to give yourself a non-slip surface to stand on.

In the colder times of the year shoes are essential, and these should be warming as well as non-slip. There are many makes available which meet both requirements. The important point is that the shoes should fit closely so that you can firmly transmit the thrust of your legs directly to the board with no intervening cushion of water or sloppiness.

When boardsailing in strong winds the body hangs out-board (right). The moment a gust eases you have to bring the centre of gravity of your body back over the board by bending your knees very quickly (far right).

Gusty winds

The anticipation of enjoying boardsailing in strong breezes is somewhat marred when the weather forecast warns of gusty freshening wind. Gusts may strike forcefully like a pneumatic hammer, and you then have great difficulty in controlling the rig. The gust may well ease equally suddenly and you are just dumped into the water. There is a special technique for sailing in such winds. Keep the weight of your body particularly low so that, when the gust strikes, you merely stretch you legs to shift your centre of gravity well to windward. This at the same time pulls the sail further to windward.

Not only does this reduce the projected sail area but it improves your leverage as you use your weight to counter the gust. If the gust eases suddenly you can bend your knees like a flash to bring your weight back over the board as quickly as possible. Should the wind drop entirely you can use knee bend in this way to the point where you are hanging beneath the boom like a limbo dancer, with your back beyond the board's centre-line. So, bending the back knee is used mainly to prevent you from falling to windward as would be inevitable if you did not bring your centre of gravity back over the board.

Remember that an offshore wind is often especially fluky because it is diverted and funnelled by the trees, houses and general unevenness of the land, all of which can cause the strength and direction of the wind to vary greatly. In fresh winds it is best therefore to find somewhere to sail where the wind blows onshore.

Planing

You will probably know already that sailing craft can be divided into two types, displacement boats and planing boats. A displacement boat is one that displaces its own weight of water and therefore always pushes its way through the water. Planing boats, on the other hand, given enough power, can lift onto the surface of the water and skim over it at higher speeds. Sailboards plane. They displace water until they reach a speed of about 8–10 knots (15–20 km/h) but beyond that point they lift out and plane.

It is planing that is so exciting when boardsailing in strong winds. The forward part of the board lifts far out of the water, the spray shoots high and the board skims over the surface like a water ski. As soon as you start to plane you will notice that the board suddenly becomes extremely stable and hardly wobbles at all. You can therefore move about on it relatively freely without it tilting. You can move quickly back and forth to make the board bear away or luff up. Take a step forward and it will bear away easily, take a step aft and it will luff up very quickly.

The actual speed at which a board changes from displacement sailing to planing depends greatly on its shape. A sailboard with a broad planing surface aft will start to plane quickly, whereas a board with a narrow stern will lift its bows sharply while the stern will squat relatively deeply in the water, and this hinders the board from planing fast. Other factors such as rocker (the curve of the underwater surface viewed from the side) and the area of the wetted surface affect the issue. More rocker makes the board manoeuvrable but delays planing. Too much wetted surface causes resistance which also hinders fast planing. Weight plays a large part too, and in general lightweight boards start to plane earlier.

Planing. The sailboard goes as fast as a water-ski, but without the need for a power boat.

Dangers in strong winds

Generally speaking there are few dangers when boardsailing inland provided you are a reasonably good swimmer and know the right-of-way rules. Apart from spectacular falls there is little that can go wrong; after all you only fall into the water! When sailing inland and the wind freshens to such an extent that you cannot hold the rig any longer, you can stand and hold the rig by the uphaul and let yourself be driven, with the sail flapping to a nearby bank. You can trail the end of the boom lightly in the water and the wind will then fill a small part of the sail. This will give you headway with the wind abeam, although slowly.

A more experienced boardsailor can also reduce the area of his sail by reefing in extremely strong winds. Just release the downhaul and push the lower part of the sail up to the boom where you make the downhaul fast to the boom fitting. This reduces the area of the sail by the amount of the triangle beneath the boom. Be careful not to pull the mast out of the mast foot when you are pushing the sail up the mast. Expert boardsailors can sail in winds up to force 7 with the sail reefed like this.

Should you be unable to reach a nearby bank with these methods you have no alternative but to use the distress signal already described (waving your arms up and down). Never panic in such a situation and, whatever you do, stay on the board because you know it is unsinkable and therefore the ideal life float.

The dangers are much greater off the coast. Sailing in a strong wind can rapidly become a disaster if, for example, some part of the board

If the wind blows too hard you can reef the sail by sliding the downhaul attachment point at the tack of the sail further up the mast, as demonstrated here on a Tandem board.

breaks when the wind is blowing off the land. You will then be driven helplessly out to sea and will be in extreme danger if no-one on land has been keeping an eye on you.

Safety rules at sea

- Do not boardsail in a strong offshore wind without assistance nearby.
- Find out from the local inhabitants the characteristics of the coastal area, ie tides, currents, sandbanks, wrecks, shipping lanes etc.
- Always wear a wet suit when boardsailing in strong winds at sea because of the great danger of hypothermia.
- Above all—always connect the rig to the board with a safetly line. If you are catapulted off, the mast foot may easily be released, and it is seldom possible to catch up with the board by swimming when the wind is strong because it is blown downwind too fast.
- Before starting out attach a line to the end of the boom so that you have a spare in case a control line parts while you are afloat.
- Check every detail of your board thoroughly before setting out in strong winds so that you are as sure as possible that nothing will break when you are sailing.

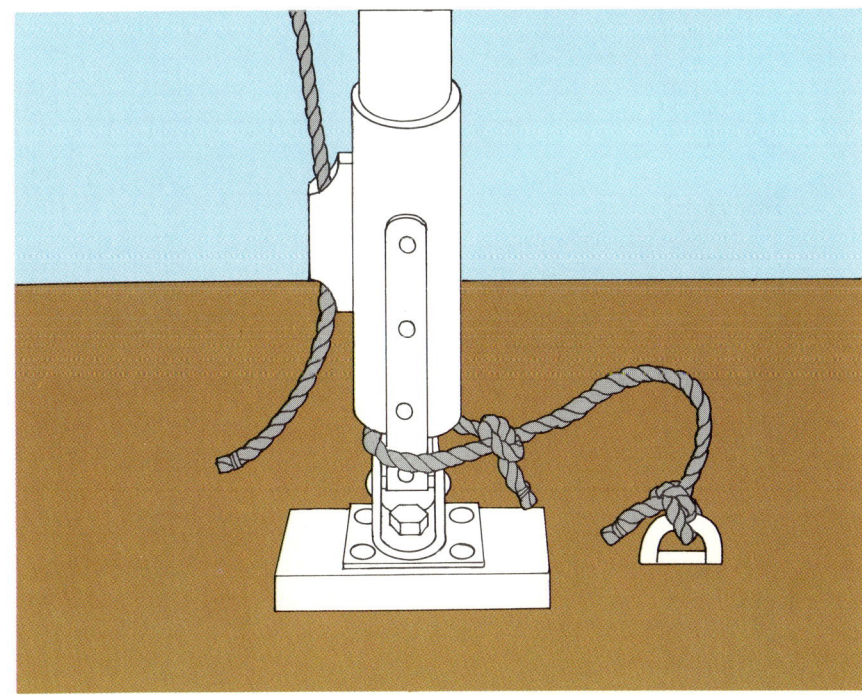

In strong winds a line between the mast and the board can be a life-saver.

Special hard weather gear

Sails

Storm sails

Keen strong wind boardsailors find that the real fun starts at force 4, but the limit comes at force 6 because even experts are barely able to support the standard rig when it blows so hard. Sailmakers have therefore produced storm sails and all-round or all-weather sails which are designed especially for heavy winds. There are two types of sails for strong winds and they differ from the normal sail mainly in that they are smaller. However the way in which the area is reduced affects board handling enormously.

In very strong wind use the all-weather sail which is smaller in area because the leech is cut concave.

Storm sail with shortened luff

The original storm sail that has been used for a number of years when boardsailing in strong winds is 3·5 m² (38 sq ft) in area which makes it about 2·00 m² (21½ sq ft) smaller than the normal sail. This area is saved by shortening the luff, and the leech therefore runs from the clew to a point some way down the mast. The upper third of the mast is only covered by the sleeve. The advantage of a short-luff storm sail is that the centre of effort is lower because a relatively large part of the sail area above the boom is missing. This saves energy because it improves the boardsailor's leverage on the boom.

However this type of storm sail has some major disadvantages. Particularly difficult are inland waters where winds are normally very fluky and gusty. The chief danger is of falling in to windward when the gust eases abruptly and there is not enough power available in this type of sail for you to be able to use it to pull your body's centre of gravity back amidships. This is due to the large reduction in area near the top of the sail. Another problem is that the greater part of the sail is just above the water where the speed of the wind is slowed considerably by friction due to the waves. Also, when the seas are very high they cause turbulence in the airstream and you have to reckon on a constant variation in wind strength, particularly low down.

This storm sail has a shortened luff and is suitable for coastal waters where the winds are steady.

The all-weather or all-round sail

The area of the all-weather sail is generally about 4·50 m² (48 sq ft) or 1·00 m² (11 sq ft) smaller than that of the normal sail. The area is reduced by cutting the leech concave instead of convex. No battens are needed to stabilise the leech, and this is an advantage because generally the first places to chafe are the batten, pockets. In strong breezes particularly, the battens are pushed forward and the elastic in the forward end of the pockets break or the stitching at the leech quickly wears through.

Another great advantage is that the all-weather sail behaves much more readily in gusts. You rarely fall to windward because the centre of effort is as high as that of a normal sail and when a gust drops suddenly there is enough power in the sail for you to pull yourself back over the board again. Knee bends are therefore more successful. The all-weather sail's greatest advantage is that the centre of effort is further forward because the area is reduced only along the leech, that is aft. This makes it much easier to get started in a strong wind and to sail through heavy gusts because the board has a less overpowering tendency to luff up.

Another effect of the centre of effort being much higher than that of the short-luff storm sail is felt when bearing away. The mast does not have to be raked so far towards the

The all-weather sail is better in gusty winds and is therefore preferable for inland sailing.

bow in order to transfer the necessary area of sail forward.

Finally, women find the all-weather sail much easier to handle because it is less heavy to pull out of the water than other sails because the water flows more easily off the concave leech. The one minor disadvantage is that you have to use slightly more strength because the centre of effort is higher by comparison with the short-luff storm sail.

Making storm sails

A normal sail is usually made of 3·8 ounce (160 gramme) sail cloth and the same cloth weight is adequate for a storm sail because relatively less total force acts on the smaller area. The sail must, however, be made much more carefully because a storm sail is intended for use in hard conditions. The mast sleeve should be reinforced at both ends with an extra layer of cloth sewn cross-wise. These doublings will last longer if they are glued before being stitched because this improves the distribution of loads over these heavily stressed areas. This is equally true of the tabling at the clew.

At the top of the mast the doubling must be worked in such a way that stress creases running into the sail are kept to a minimum. It is best to extend the sail on the rig before you buy it to check that it sets smoothly.

The sail should also have extra protection against chafe at the mast top to prevent the mast poking through after a time. A storm sail should also have two gaps in the mast sleeve so that the boom height can be

adapted to the individual. Children will then also be able to use it. Check too that the mast sleeve is not too wide—12 cm (4½ ins) is the maximum—because a wider sleeve would collect far too much water inside it and make it virtually impossible to raise the rig out of the water in strong winds.

Harnesses

Trapeze harnesses have long been used by dinghy sailors, and have been adapted for boardsailing. The harness is a device designed to save effort when the boardsailor is hanging out to windward by connecting him to the boom, and is now by far the most popular aid for strong wind boardsailing. Since the Hawaiians introduced the harness at the 1976 World Championships boardsailors have no longer been content to depend on muscle power alone when hanging from the boom. Ingenious designers have been working out a number of different systems to make it easier to hook on, to make the harness more comfortable and, above all, to make sure that they are as safe as possible.

However many strong wind boardsailors still feel that the best system of all is to be physically fit and not to use a harness at all! This is right of course, particularly when boardsailing on reservoirs and flooded quarries where the distances covered are so short. A harness in such waters is quite unnecessary.

It is a very different matter when it comes to covering long stretches at sea, and perhaps also where one has to sail in a strong offshore wind. A boardsailor can be carried miles offshore by the wind and current and is then faced with a seemingly endless sail back close-hauled which calls for more strength than is possessed by even the toughest of sailors. A harness is then not just an aid to strong wind boardsailing but in some circumstances can well be a life-saver. In almost all the photographs of Hawaiians, whose Hawaii harness was the first practical sailboard harness to be developed, they are seen to be wearing a harness, but they hardly ever hook themselves on. They wear them only for safety, in case the wind shifts or freshens violently, or in case they get cramp. It may be largely psychological, but the feeling is that the harness can be used as a sort of safety belt if the worst comes to the worst.

In any case safety is always the most important factor and you must therefore check that your harness can be unhooked easily when you fall so that you are not catapulted onto the board by the rig in a strong gust. The more popular systems and how they function are described below.

A harness can save effort when boardsailing in strong steady winds. It takes some time to get used to and there are various types on the market.

The Hawaii harness

The boom is pulled towards you briefly and a downwards-opening hook on the chest strap of the harness is passed over a rope attached to the boom. Before tacking or gybing, or when falling, you have to pull yourself towards the boom to disconnect the harness, and the rope then automatically drops out of the hook. The problem is that if the gust strikes very suddenly it is not always possible to pull the boom in equally quickly to release yourself. In a catapult fall you may even be twisted round the boom in such a way that the rope twists round the hook and you cannot then free yourself, which is obviously dangerous.

Be very careful therefore to ensure that a Hawaii harness has a quick release buckle so that you can get free if, for example, you find yourself submerged and under the sail.

The Charchulla Channel system

The idea of saving your strength when boardsailing was actually first put into practice not by the Hawaiians but by the Bremen twins Manfred and Jürgen Charchulla. In 1975 they were the first to cross the English Channel on a sailboard and devised a fitting to relieve their muscles when covering long distances in fresh winds. A broad leather strap is buckled around the hips and a track is screwed to the boom. An adjustable line attached to the strap is made fast in a cam cleat in the track on the boom, and the end is held by the sheet hand. To release the harness before

tacking, gybing or falling the sheet hand just pulls the rope out of the cleat. This system is very safe because you are always able to release yourself from the boom, but the disadvantage is that one hand has to let go of the boom to cleat the rope.

Sailorsurf adjustable hook

Another method of hanging from the boom was thought out by the Dutchman Richard Stigchen. A hinged hook is hung over the boom and is attached to the chest harness with a line. When you fall your sheet hand pulls a line which operates on a small sleeve to disengage the hook from the boom. The system is very safe but as with the Charchulla system you have to take one hand off the boom to hook on. After you have released yourself you then need two hands to reassemble the hook and sleeve.

Sailorsurf moulded rubber glove/hooks

An idea devised by Dorothee Bürger from Darmstadt consists of a harness and curved hard moulded rubber gloves. The boardsailor slips his hands into these gloves which are connected to the belt by lines. When setting off you just grip the boom and hang out, about three-quarters of the load being taken by the non-slip gloves and the belt. In dangerous situations you merely remove your hands from the boom. A very safe system.

Harnesses. *Above left*: Hawaii harness; *Bottom left*: Charchulla Channel harness; *Top right*: Sailorsurf system; *Bottom right*: Sailorsurf system with gloves.

Whatever harness a strong wind boardsailor chooses he must ensure that it is safe in a fall. He must be able to free himself from the boom. It takes quite some time to get used to a harness so they should always be tried our first in lighter breezes before being used in a strong wind.

The daggerboard

Storm daggerboard

Anyone who wants to enjoy boardsailing to the full in strong winds certainly ought to take a good look at his daggerboard. Many manufacturers now produce accurately streamlined plastic daggerboards which would be hard to improve, though good mahogany or teak daggerboards have an even better strength to weight ratio at higher cost.

But what makes a good daggerboard? The main factor is the profile of the cross-section. The best daggerboard is shaped on both sides like the upper surface of an aeroplane's wing. It should have a rounded leading edge, will be thickest about a third of the way back and then taper smoothly to a fine trailing edge. A good chord to thickness ratio is about 10 to 1.

As Hawaiian Larry Stanley jumps you can clearly see the shape of the Hawaii daggerbaord which is raked well aft.

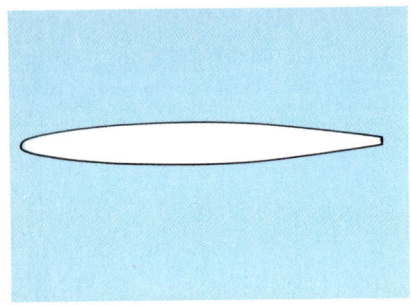

The cross section of a daggerboard with an optimum aerofoil shape should be roughly like this.

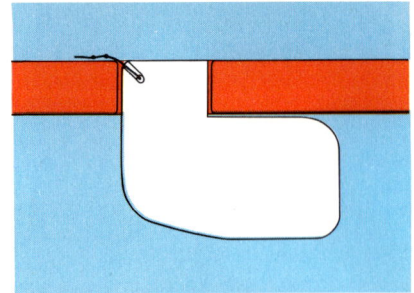

The Charchulla daggerboard provides almost too much directional stability for use in high waves.

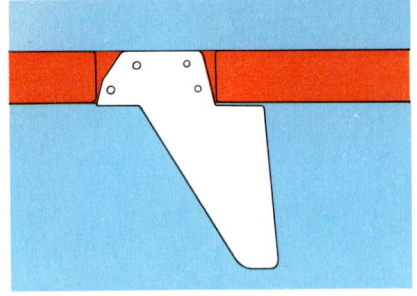

The Hawaii daggerboard is ideal for surfsailing but it will not allow the board to sail close to the wind.

A streamlined daggerboard is particularly important when boardsailing in fresh winds because minimum resistance to the water flow is essential if you are to sail fast. A section as described above offers least resistance.

Check, too, that your daggerboard is really smooth because even protruding wooden dowels that have not been planed flat will brake your speed enormously. The size of the daggerboard will of course considerably affect your board's performance in fresh winds because, as you know, the board does not normally sail absolutely straight through the water but at a slight angle owing to the fact that it makes some leeway. This means that the direction of water flow is not from dead ahead and parallel to the daggerboard but at a slight angle to it. This angle of attack, or leeway angle, results in pressure to leeward and suction to windward of the daggerboard, producing a side force lifting the board to windward just as the wing of an aeroplane, or the sail itself, generates lift. The faster the board moves the faster the water flows past and the greater the side force. This leads to the well known 'capsize fall' which is described more fully in the next chapter.

The best way to avoid this typical strong wind fall is to decrease the area of the daggerboard so as to reduce the side force, and this is why storm daggerboards of various shapes have been designed, all being smaller than the normal daggerboard.

Another characteristic of a storm daggerboard is that when fitted into the trunk the lateral area lies considerably further aft than that of a normal daggerboard. Consequently the CLR, around which the sailboard pivots, will also be further aft and this makes the board less eager to luff up into the wind which is a particular problem in fresh winds. It also makes it easier to take off in a strong wind.

Another argument in favour of the storm daggerboard is because the bow lifts quite far above the water when planing, sometimes even as far back as the leading edge of the daggerboard. A great deal of turbulence arises at this point and this too increases the likelihood of a capsize fall. It is very noticeable how much more quietly the sailboard slips through the water with a daggerboard lying further aft.

The first storm daggerboard was developed by Manfred and Jürgen Charchulla. It was a flat piece of wood which had to be inserted into the slot from below and shifted the lateral area well aft, but it was virtually impossible to streamline it satisfactorily. Since then the Americans, in particular, have designed dozens of different types and each boardsailor swears by the shape of the one he uses. One of the best-known is the Hawaii surf daggerboard which is of small area and is raked well aft.

The great disadavantage common to all storm daggerboards is that you cannot sail to windward so efficiently because you make more leeway due to the reduction in lateral area. Be sure, then, that your daggerboard is large enough to allow you to sail reasonably close to the wind. Otherwise, although you may be enjoying yourself whizzing back and forth on one broad reach after another, you may be unable to return to your departure point. When surf-sailing, which we discuss in a later chapter, the small daggerboard has another advantage. It allows you to drift sideways on a wave, its lower thrust allowing you to slide sideways across the back of a wave.

A really keen strong wind boardsailor will undoubtedly need a special daggerboard for every type of sailing; a racing daggerboard for light winds and sailing to windward, a storm daggerboard with its smaller lateral area further aft for strong winds and shallow waters, and a surf daggerboard with a very much smaller lateral area to enable you to drift sideways in waves. But take care because, with the surf daggerboard, you can never sail really close to the wind. It can therefore only be recommended for use when the surf is about a metre high.

This pivoted centreboard can be raised and lowered and is therefore suitable both for windward work and for surfsailing.

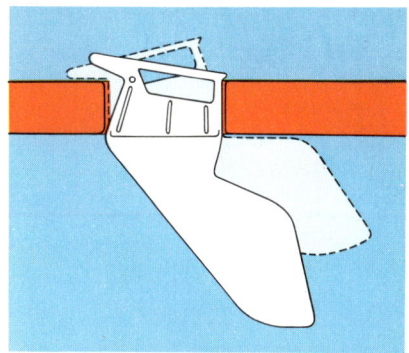

Pivoting centreboard

The most practical solution to the daggerboard problem when boardsailing in strong winds is the pivoting centreboard. Pressure from the foot moves it from the normal vertical position, to a new position, raked aft and partly raised so that you get the same effect as the storm and surf daggerboards in one. When it is vertical the CLR is in the same place as when using a racing daggerboard, but the lateral area is slightly smaller. In the raised position the lateral area is still smaller, the CLR moves aft and the board draws much less water. Most centreboards pivot and are operated by foot so as to avoid your having to bend down, which can be difficult, particularly when the waves are running high.

When the centreboard is down in its vertical position:

- In strong winds you can sail to windward just as well as when using a normal daggerboard.
- You can run into shallow water, or even up onto the shore, without raising it first because it will automatically pivot up and aft when it touches the ground. Nor will the trunk be damaged because the shock is widely distributed over the board.

When the centreboard is raised:

- The board draws very little water, and this makes it easier to get under way in surf and in shallow waters.

- Hydroplaning does not occur at high speeds due to the lateral area being smaller and the CLR being shifted further aft (see chapter on capsize falls).
- The board's tendency to luff up sharply when getting under way in strong winds is less marked because the CLR is further aft.
- It is easier to drift sideways in high waves because the lateral area is smaller.

Naturally a lifting daggerboard operated by foot on a pivot must protrude above the slot and this is inconvenient because it does so just where the boardsailor stands. A further disadvantage is that when it is raised it is no longer perfectly streamlined.

Courses in strong winds

Close-hauled

The wind is offshore, force 5–6, and you are thoroughly enjoying yourself speeding over the water on a couple of broad reaches. Suddenly you realise with astonishment that you are a mile or two away from your departure point and that you have a very long way to beat back against the wind. Always remind yourself before starting off that, depending on the strength of the wind, half an hour's broad reaching is equivalent to about three hour's to windward so never sail too far away from the shore in off-shore winds. If the wind shifts while you are out and you are forced to cover a long stretch close-hauled

When your forearms get tired you can crook the wishbone in your elbow or under your armpit.

there are ways of making this less arduous. First there is the harness which has already been described. If you have no harness always keep your arms fully stretched when on the wind to avoid becoming exhausted too quickly. Small alterations to your course in response to wind shifts can best be made by pushing your shoulders forward or back, or by slightly turning your body. If you feel after a time as if your arms have been stretched out of their sockets, which really means that your strength is beginning to fail, change your grip more frequently or use the 'old man's grip' by hooking the boom into your elbow or under your armpit. This takes the load off your hands, even if only for a short while.

If you stay on one tack for a long time and reach the point where you simply have no strength left to keep on leaning out on the boom it is best to go about to give your forearms a brief rest. Do not take too much time over it though, or you will drift downwind and lose a lot of the distance that you have gained to windward. If the wind freshens so much that you simply cannot hold on to the rig, rake the mast really far to windward when getting under way and only sheet in the sail a little way, just to the point where it is still lifting all along the luff. The wind will then only fill the sail along the leech, near the end of the boom, while the forward part of the sail will shake. You can make reasonable progress to windward with the sail spilling a lot of wind like this if you find yourself in trouble.

Do not attempt to point closer than about 45° to the wind when it is blowing hard. If you tried to point higher you would have to sheet in the sail over the stern and would lose forward speed. Remember too to allow for leeway in fresh winds because the stronger the wind the more leeway will you make. If you wish to sail directly to a point on land always aim a few degrees to windward of it.

Beam reaching and broad reaching

All that has been said already about strong wind boardsailing is relevvant to sailing on broad and beam reaches. It is in this arc, between 90° and 135° to the wind, that you will most want to sail. Whizzing over a smooth mountain lake on a reach is tremendous fun, and it is on this course that sea sailing is also at its most exciting.

No special skills are required beyond those you have already learnt, but it is the waves that become really significant in fresh winds and their size will depend on whether you are sailing on a large or small expanse of water. When you are on a beam reach the wind-raised waves will be travelling in a direction that is roughly at 90° to your course. This makes it difficult for you to steer a straight course because you will be continually lifted up on their crests only to slip down the backs of the waves into the troughs. So bear away slightly on the face, to make full use of the thrust of the wave, and then luff up a little on the crest so that you can plane down into the trough.

On a broad reach you will generally be sailing in the same direction as the wind waves and at a slight angle to them. You can often ride on one wave for minutes at a time. If you intend to do this have a good look around first and select one of the highest waves. Once you have got to grips with it you will be able to swing about on its face like a skier, bearing away to plane down towards the trough and then luffing up slightly so that you are lifted up the face again. If the wind is strong enough you can go on roller-coasting like this for as long as you please. You may find that you are sailing rather faster than the wave is travelling, in other words, over 23 km/h (13 knots). Enjoy yourself!

Broad reaching is obviously a lot of fun! When sailing in this direction the board travels fastest.

Running

Now it becomes more difficult. When you bear away from a broad reach you come to a course which even the best boardsailors in the world find the most tricky. Running in strong winds is always a very dicey business.

The first problem is bearing away and, initially, this will probably cause your many a swim. Why should this happen? As you have already learnt you rake the mast forward to bear away and simultaneously sheet in the sail slightly. The board turns away from the wind and—immediately, you reach the critical point! At that instant the apparent wind suddenly shifts further aft and laminar flow accelerates or sets in over the upper part of the sail which had been doing little or no work before hand. This causes an equally sudden rise in the pressure of the wind on the sail, and the centre of effort also shifts higher. Not only have you got to counter more wind pressure but your leverage is worse. The consequence is that the rig takes charge and swings forward at an angle with great force inevitably tossing you off the board. This is called catapult falling and we describe how you can avoid such falls in the next chapter.

When you bear away on to a run keep the centre of gravity of your body really low to minimise balancing problems.

Always think first and bear away deliberately, moving slowly and with concentration. Remember that you must keep on sheeting out the sail as the wind blows from further and further aft. This is what most people forget when they are bearing away.

React to the increase in pressure instantly by easing out your sheet hand and help the board to turn with your feet, forcefully thrusting the board round and away from the wind by putting your weight on your front foot which can be positioned some way forward of the mast step. Your back foot is used only to help you balance.

When your board has borne away almost to a dead run you will notice a sudden reduction of pressure on the sail. This is because laminar flow over the sail has ceased and, instead of a driving force being developed owing to suction to leeward and pressure to windward, you are simply pushed downwind like a leaf by wind which acts only on the windward side of the sail.

Meanwhile you change the position of your feet considerably, turning your body towards the direction in which you are heading so that you look towards the bow through the window in the sail and at the same time place both feet near the daggerboard trunk. The harder the wind is blowing the further aft will you have to shift your weight.

Once you have reached this point you will find that a run is not so very difficult provided you keep your weight evenly distributed between your feet, and counter the see-saw effect of the waves instantly by pushing down slightly to port or starboard. It is also important to keep your body's centre of gravity as low as possible so that the force of the wind is unable to whip you forward off your feet. This will also make it less likely that the waves can shake you off balance.

Best of all is to bring your centre of gravity down and aft by kneeling on the board. Bend one knee, preferably the one on the same side as your mast hand, and stretch the other behind you. In our experience this is the surest position when running because you can keep your balance well and also stand up quickly.

In a very strong wind you may need to bring your centre of gravity still closer to the board and it is then best to sit back on the board with your legs stretched out in front of you towards the mast foot. In this sitting position you have to pull the rig back quite far over the board and this considerably reduces the projected

When the wind is even stronger you should kneel or sit on the board when running. A strong wind can hardly be mastered in any other way on this direction of sailing.

sail area. You can even go so far as to lie on your back with the boom at arm's length above you, but then there is little chance of altering course suddenly or adjusting to a wind shift because you are far less mobile.

It is more difficult to steer the board on a run in strong winds than on any other point of sailing because it is so hard to keep your balance. To alter course to starboard you tilt the rig to port, and vice versa, and must use your feet at the same time to avoid losing your balance. The board responds slowly at first when you tilt the rig, but after it has luffed a little way it will suddenly react and turn extremely quickly. To steer a straight course on a run it is best to keep the boom parallel to the surface of the water. The mast will be pointing out slightly to one side of the board and the rig will be in a position of balance.

Whatever the outcome of your first attempts at running never forget that expert boardsailors also find it difficult, not only because so much strength is needed but because maximum concentration and perfect balance are vital.

Tacking and gybing in strong winds

Tacking

It is as essential to be able to tack as to have water on which to sail. In a strong wind, particularly, it is all too easy to be tempted to cover a mile or so broad reaching, and you are then faced with a long sail-back close-hauled. This immediately means trouble for anyone who has not mastered the art of tacking, especially if he cannot even turn the board. There are people, of course, who deliberately fall into the water when they want to change tacks; they push the board round while they are swimming, climb on it again and set off on the opposite tack. You would naturally prefer to do it better, and not just better but above all faster.

For example you need to change tacks quickly to win races, to avoid a ship or some other obstacle that you have sighted too late, or perhaps just for show. Above all it is vital to be able to tack quickly and surely to avoid endangering yourself or other people on the water. Various methods of changing tacks have evolved, depending on the reason for tacking, the type of board, the strength of the wind and the height of the waves.

When learning you discovered how unstable you were when shuffling round to the other side of the board. The quicker you cross forward of the mast and can again use the stabilising effect of wind pressure, in other words, use the rig to help you keep your balance, the less likely you are to fall in.

When racing the ability to tack surely and quickly is an absolute necessity. The racing rules often call for a sailboard on port tack to make a rapid avoidance of one or more boards on starboard tack, and the only way might be a rapid change of tack.

Taking is largely a question of practice and either improving your skill or perhaps developing a new technique. The different methods

A Jump tack

1. This is a Jump tack. To free weight from the bow, shift your back foot aft and transfer your weight on to it.

2. Quickly rake the mast aft. Your front foot says near the mast and the board shoots into the wind.

3. Your sheet hand grabs the mast, which is still raked aft, above the boom. The board is turning fast.

4. Now take two steps and turn your body round the mast.

have been refined through the years as a result of racing sailboards and the question is, which method is best? The *jump, jet* or *duck* tack? There is no quick answer because too many factors are involved including the type of board, the strength of the wind, the waves and the reason for tacking which could be to give way (sudden) or for some tactical reason in a race (deliberate), quite apart from freestyle tacking (elegant) and tacking in strong winds (survival). A few basic comments can nevertheless be made:

- A short board like the 'Windsurfer' generally turns more quickly than a long one, just as you can turn faster on a mogul-covered piste using short skis. Short boards are always more suitable for freestyle competition.
- Even an extra 30 cm (12 ins) length is a disadvantage, and a 'Windglider', for example, requires a completely different tacking technique. It is impossible to do a jet tack, which involves moving your weight aft and pivoting round on the skeg, because the stern squats and the relatively high rails of the board thrust sideways against the water which brakes the turning movement.
- The turning ability of the board depends largely on the skeg. Freestyle experts cut practically all of the skeg away to get the board to turn more quickly but it is doubtful whether it is wise to use a shortened sawn-off skeg for all round sailing. The disadvantage immediately becomes apparent when broad reaching because directional stability will be poor and you have to keep on correcting your course when the board yaws to windward and leeward.
- The distance between daggerboard and skeg is important too. The smaller the gap the faster will the board turn, but this is something you cannot alter because no board has yet been made with an adjustable skeg.

What really decides your tacking method is whether you are racing, boardsailing in strong winds or freestyle sailing. For freestyle you need to change tacks to show off with a lightning quick turn and as elegantly as possible whereas, when racing, the aim is not to slacken speed or lose distance gained to windward, and indeed to gain time and distance if possible.

A tack can be considered to be completed when the sail is full on the new tack but, owing to the unique design of the sailboard with its mobile rig, it is possible to jump over to the opposite side before the bow has passed right through the eye of the wind. You will then be standing with your sail backed to windward of the centreline and, although the sail is full and the tack completed, your board is just lying still, making no headway in the water. To spectators

5. At the same time throw the mast forward past your body.

6. Your free hand is ready to catch hold of the boom.

7. Your mast hand rapidly grabs the boom and your sheet hand hardens in the sail with a single tug while you move your body aft and to windward to lift the bow.

8. Off you go on the new tack!

it appears that you have tacked unbelievably quickly but in fact it is only your change of position to the new side that is so fast. To tack like this in a race would be completely wrong, and a spectator's wry comment during a freestyle competition in Sardinia, 'there can be no quicker way of putting on the brakes' makes the point perfectly.

Then there is the wind strength to consider. Obviously tacking in light breezes requires a very different technique to that used in strong winds. When the wind is light you should turn smoothly without sheeting the sail in too far. You rake the rig aft and only pull the sail back slightly beyond the centreline at the last moment as the bow comes head to wind. When you move over to the new side you should not jerk or rock the board. Grasp the *mast* with your mast hand at boom height and pull it

A Jet tack

1. This is a Jet, or fast, tack.

2. The rig is raked extremely far aft to swing the board right through the eye of the wind.

3. To accelerate this swing you jump about 18 inches (half a metre) aft of the daggerboard trunk and force the stern round with both feet.

4. As soon as the board shoots through the wind you change sides.

A Duck tack

1. To duck tack under the boom the essential is that the board should not merely turn head to wind.

2. It must swing through the eye of the wind.

3. The rig is raked aft and you move both feet slightly further aft at the same time to accelerate the swing, just as when jet tacking.

4. Instead of running round forward of the mast you back the sail for a moment so that you are in effect standing on what will be the leeward side of the board.

past your body. You then catch hold of the boom on what is now the windward side with your free hand. Using this 'cross-grip' method you catch hold of the *mast* instead of supporting the rig with the uphaul or the boom, and this has proved to be much faster in winds varying from force 2 to force 7. It is up to you whether you hold the mast with your mast or sheet hand.

In strong winds with these methods the major difference is that the board turns quicker. Above force 2 or 3 you can swing the board round even faster and without losing way, but this must naturally always be matched to your own speed and skill when changing sides.

. You have to take several eps to get round the mast ecause there is further to go.

6. The actions with your hands are exactly the same as when jump tacking.

7. So is the method of getting moving on the new tack.

8. Close-hauled again.

. Now throw the sail forward ad into the wind. Your sheet nd releases the port boom.

6. Then duck beneath the sail while your sheet hand grasps the starboard boom.

7. Simultaneously your mast hand releases the port boom. Stand and turn your body quickly towards the sail.

8. Lean the rig forward to get moving in the same way as when jump or jet tacking.

Gybing

Whereas gybing a sailing boat is generally more tricky than tacking it is relatively easy to gybe a sailboard because, instead of the boom slamming right over from one side to the other with its outboard end pointing towards the wind, it is just swung round over the bow and sheeted in on the new side. It is only when you want to lose as few valuable seconds as possible, say during a race, that the running gybe, or catapult gybe, can be used by anybody who is quick on his feet.

Running or catapult gybe

Instead of swinging the sail gently round the bow in the normal way it is thrown over to the opposite side. Suppose that you are on a beam reach and have to gybe round a mark in the course. You rake the mast to windward and forward to make the board bear away while your sheet hand pulls in sharply to increase the pressure briefly, which considerably speeds the board's turn. It is absolutely vital not to lose your balance at this stage. There is always a considerable risk of falling when the board bears away towards a dead run. As the wind direction shifts further and further aft laminar flow suddenly ceases and wind pressure on

A catapult, or running gybe is shown left to right, top row followed by bottom row. After bearing away onto a run the sail is literally thrown round, aided by the pressure of the wind, onto the opposite side.

the sail suddenly drops. You sink back into the water slowly and the rig subsides on top of you.

To avoid this you must keep your weight over the centre of the board as soon as it starts to bear away. You will find it easier to keep your balance if your weight is low, so bend your back knee to bring your centre of gravity right down.

When gybing normally the latest moment to swing the sail over onto the opposite side is just before you reach the point when you are on a run, but with a running gybe you delay this and keep on bearing away until you are running dead before the wind, standing upright now with the mast to windward, the boom horizontal and the sail straight across the board.

Only now do you start the gybe proper by raking the mast extremely far to windward to make the board bear away fruther, at the same time using the feet to help it turn. If turning to port you turn your body and bring your front foot, which will be your right foot, well aft and push on the port rail of the board to make it swing round. You move your left foot aft when turning to starboard. Thus when gybing and turning to port the weight of your body will be on the port rail aft, and when gybing and turning to starboard it will be on the starboard rail aft.

Your mast hand now pulls the boom further to windward and aft at the same time. The stern of the board will have already passed through the wind direction but the sail will still be on the original tack.

Then starts the actual 'catapulting' action. Your sheet hand throws the boom forward with a jerk, quickly grabs the mast above the boom and pulls it past your body to the new windward side. At the same time your mast hand drops the boom and grabs hold of the other side of the wishbone to become the sheet hand on the new tack. While catapulting the sail over both feet should be well aft of the daggerboard slot, but you now move them back to their normal position for a beam reach. You have completed the gybe and the sail is trimmed correctly for your new course.

This all happens so quickly that each phase merges into the next and, because you cannot pause briefly as when gybing normally, you are unlikely to avoid falling at your first attempts. Do not be discouraged however because you will only really find gybing fun when you can do a catapult gybe successfully.

Stop gybe

You have an emergency! An obstacle appears suddenly and without warning, say another boat, or a swimmer. You just had not seen it before, perhaps because the window in your sail was too small or because you had shut your eyes for a few moments from sheer pleasure. There are two ways of stopping your board dead. You can simply let the sail drop into the water as beginners do. It will then act like a sea anchor and bring the board to a halt. Alternatively you can use the much more elegant stop gybe which will stop your board in an instant. You can then turn the board on to the opposite tack if you want. If you merely wish to stop you naturally need not turn the board completely round; you might alter course to a run instead.

This is how to do a stop gybe. When sailing on the wind or with the wind abeam you suddenly thrust the sail back against the wind. This forces it towards you and you find that you are standing to leeward of the sail. It is important that your sheet hand should be the first to act, thrusting the sail aback. Stretching this arm right out will stop the board immediately. Then pull the sail slightly to windward with your mast hand but keep pushing the rig against the wind with your sheet hand. This will make the sailboard turn rapidly and you have to shift your feet quickly. There is a danger that the forward part of the board may then bury under the waves and you would not then be able to control the turning movement, so let go with your sheet hand and thrust the rig towards the bow only with your mast hand until the board has turned round completely.

You will find this useful later on, particularly at the start of a race when you can manoeuvre yourself into the correct position by alternately sheeting in and backing your sail slightly.

To stop dead (a stop gybe) push the sail hard aback against the wind. This is called backing the sail. The board will stop immediately.

Strong-wind falls

No strong wind boardsailor can escape full-blooded falls. We are not talking now about those gentle flops into the water that are part of every learner's repertoire in the early stages, but of falls such as capsize and catapult falls that can be anticipated but are nevertheless unavoidable. Their names given the game away: they are fast and violent.

When sailing in strong winds there are moments, for example during bearing away, when the boom forcibly drags you forward, when you find that your back foot is lifted off the board even though you use your last ounce of strength trying to stand firm. In that fraction of a second you know you will be catapulted through the air while the mast crashes down violently on the board or into the water. You still just have time to let go of the boom and flop back into the water, but we feel this is hardly a skilful way of parting with the board. If we are going to abandon ship let us do so with dignity!

Several of the most frequent falls are described in the following paragraphs, together with suggestions as to how you can try to avoid them.

Falls are very much part of boardsailing in strong winds. People who never fall will never become real expert boardsailors.

Diving fall

This is particularly likely to happen when you are reaching or running down a wave and the front part of the board buries its way beneath the surface and keeps on diving. Once it has dived deep enough it will probably suddenly shoot sideways and upwards, and you will generally be thrown overboard.

Diving falls are particularly likely to occur if your board has insufficient rocker, in other words, if it does not curve up sufficiently at the bow. This is why the Hawaiians have bent the bows of their boards up by applying heat, but please do not attempt to do this yourself without some experience. It is better to take advice from an expert sailboard supplier. Diving falls can be avoided by correct handling too. When sailing fast down into a wave trough move both feet further aft to lift the tip of the board, and luff slightly to sail at an angle to the face of your wave. This keeps the nose of the board clear of the critical point—the back of the wave ahead.

Windward flop

You are particularly likely to fall to leeward in waters such as mountain lakes where the direction of the wind may shift 180° in a gust or alternatively, stop altogether for a moment. You may be sailing close-hauled when a gust of this sort strikes (or the wind dies) and you will then immediately splash down to leeward. Generally you have no chance of taking any avoiding action and the sail will fall on top of you. Sometimes you will find that the wind shifts slightly less violently and you can then try to counter it and avoid a fall by pulling the sail back towards you over the centreline of the board. This will slow you down considerably and you may either have to tack or bear away too.

Catapult fall

This is undoubtedly one of the most gymnastic ways of leaving your board. It happens in strong winds wherever you may be sailing, regardless of the height of the waves or which make of sailboard you are using, but it is most common just after getting moving when you want to bear away to sail at maximum speed. In order to start you rake the mast slightly forward and gently sheet in the sail at the same time. Rake the mast further forward, the board and rig start to turn away from the wind and immediately the critical moment arrives.

The direction of the apparent wind shifts further aft and there is a sudden increase in laminar flow over the upper part of the sail which formerly was not full or barely drawing. This causes wind pressure on the sail to increase and the centre of effort to move higher in the sail. The result is

A real windward flop. An expert boardsailor would probably have jumped and twisted himself half round (a half-twist) or bent his hips.

that you can no longer counter the extra pressure of the wind on the sail by strength and body weight alone. The rig crashes forward with enormous force and extremely suddenly while all you can do is to fly after it. We must repeat that no strong wind boardsailor has avoided such falls.

But what can you do to prevent this happening? First remember the basic rule that the harder the wind blows the more must you rake the mast to windward and not just forwards. This reduces the area of sail projected and consequently wind pressure is also slightly reduced. Never bear away without first thinking what you are going to do and then act slowly and with concentration, deliberately raking the mast to windward and forward. Your sheet hand must be very sensitively used. If you feel that the sail is pulling too hard ease it out slightly but be sure to keep the rig raked well to windward. Remember too that you must always ease out the sail in any case when you bear away because the wind blows from further aft. Shift your centre of gravity well aft before bearing away and bend your legs, leaning back against the wind to counter the increased wind force with the weight of your body.

Capsize fall

Have you experienced this? You have worked some way to windward, rested a while and are looking forward to an exciting broad reach back. You get going, but not for long because the board does something that you probably have never seen before. One of the rails lifts up suddenly and irresistably and whips right over—that is a capsize fall.

All strong wind boardsailors have had to battle with this and, for a long time, no one knew why it happened. We know now that the reason is the daggerboard. It starts to lead a life of

A classic catapult fall. The boardsailor bears away without easing out the sail at the right moment. He is suddenly whipped forward with enormous force. The only hope is to let go of the boom and fall in with dignity.

its own beneath the water in a strong wind.

The water streams past both sides of the daggerboard, which should be perfectly streamlined. However a sailboard does not sail quite straight through the water but at a slight angle due to leeway and the water therefore strikes the daggerboard at a small angle. In consequence the water particles have to travel a greater distance along one side of the daggerboard than along the other. Pressure is therefore lower on the former side and causes suction in just the same way as there is suction on the lee side of your sail. The faster you move through the water the greater the suction and the more forcibly will the daggerboard try to lift towards the surface of the water. This is hydroplaning.

Furthermore at high speeds the front part of the board, almost back as far as the leading edge of the daggerboard, is lifted above the surface. The turbulence arising from the board's bow wave also affects the daggerboard and encourages this tendency to capsize.

The smaller the area of your daggerboard the smaller the resulting hydrodynamic forces. Raising the daggerboard part way does reduce the area but the disadvantage is that the top then protrudes above the board just where you stand. Lifting centreboards and the various types of storm daggerbaord make a capsize fall less likely, but the best solution is to remove the daggerboard entirely on a broad reach or run.

A capsize fall is almost unavoidable at high speeds if you use a full-sized daggerboard. Often you get some warning because the rail of the board starts to lift. You can either slow down by sheeting out the sail, or you can take a ducking.

Boardsailing without a daggerboard

There is only one real problem when it comes to riding the waves without a daggerboard, but it is one of the greatest. This is—getting started. You know already that the board becomes much less stable when the daggerboard is removed, and this is more so when a strong wind raises waves, and these will be choppy, steep or long depending on the area where you are sailing. But once you have succeeded in getting under way you will be surprised to find that the board becomes extraordinarily stable, does not yaw off course and planes at maximum speed down into the wave troughs while a water fountain spurts high out of the daggerboard slot. There is no doubt that this is a tremendous sensation.

Great skill—tremendous thrills! Without a daggerboard you can enjoy the great sensation of wave-riding. But getting started without a daggerboard is one of the most difficult problems to solve.

Quite apart from enjoyment it is absolutely essential to be able to sail with no daggerboard on the reaching and running legs of a race when the wind is strong. In the Windsurfer World Championships at Bendor in 1975 the Americans walked off with all the prizes because they sailed away from the Europeans on all downwind courses. The Americans simply hung their daggerboards over their arms while the Europeans struggled from one capsize fall to the next.

But to start without a daggerboard the first essential is that your balance must be really good. Place your front foot just forward of the mast foot, your back foot at the aft end of the daggerboard trunk and turn the board slightly towards a broad reaching position by moving the uphaul to rake the mast slightly forward. Your mast hand reaches over the uphaul and supports the rig by the boom, allowing the sail to shake freely. Now bend down and pull the daggerboard out by its strap or cord, hanging it on the forearm or elbow of the sheet hand. Your mast hand then pulls the rig past your chest, raking it so far to windward that the boom end points upwards at an angle. It is essential to pull the sail right over to windward because you must bear away the moment you start to gather way. Now grab the boom with your sheet hand, sheet in vigorously and simultaneously use your weight to counter the wind pressure by leaning well aft, using your front foot, which is still ahead of the mast, to thrust the bow around and away from the wind. The board is encouraged to bear away by raking the mast further forward and to windward while sheeting in.

Suddenly you realise that the board is planing, speed continues to increase and you start tearing over the water.

You can now move your foot behind the mast and shift your weight further aft to prevent the bow of the board burying under the waves. The water will be fountaining high through the slot but the board will be relatively stable and you can change your position confidently until you find the best place to stand.

You can broad reach without a daggerboard in winds up to force 7 and will be sailing at maximum speed because, with no daggerboard, friction is at a minimum. You will be travelling so fast that you will even over-take the waves. When you sail down into a trough, shift your weight further aft to lift the tip of the board which will now have to plane up the back of the wave ahead. Sheet in the sail at the same time to increase the wind pressure.

While scorching over the water at high speed the daggerboard will be bumping about on your sheet arm. If it hits the water it may twist the chord round your arm and this can be painful. Your daggerboard may already have a strap instead but, if not, replace the cord with a strap that is fairly broad.

When you are trying to get started you sometimes find that the board simply refuses to bear away and you are driven to leeward with your sail sheeted in. The only remedy—and it cannot be repeated too often—is to rake the mast really far to *windward*, sheet the sail in hard and at the same moment thrust the bow round with your front foot. The board will accelerate very rapidly without a daggerboard but at full speed, and particularly surfing down waves the wind pressure on the sail will ease off.

In strong winds you can luff up about as far as a beam reach without a daggerboard but, with the best will in the world, you can head up no closer because the lateral area of the fin is too small to prevent the board making leeway. For this reason never set out from a beach without taking a daggerboard with you. Without it you will probably be unable to return to your departure point.

Practise starting without a daggerboard in rather lighter winds at first to get the feel of it, but winds under force 4 are too light. The board will not plane and will be very unstable.

After a little practice you will find you can start without a daggerboard. The frictional resistance of the trunk always acts as a slight brake. So you can plane even faster if you stop up the daggerboard slot to prevent the water spraying through it. A good method is to cut a piece of flexible polyethylene foam to the exact size of the slot. Push this in place when you hang the daggerboard over your arm. The piece of polyethylene foam can easily be stowed in a wet suit or even in a pair of bathing shorts when you are sailing to windward.

Various designs of skegs have different effects on handling.

The skeg

The skeg has barely been mentioned until now. As a beginner you learnt that the skeg is responsible for keeping a steady course but now, when boardsailing in strong winds and, above all, when sailing without a daggerboard it becomes far more important because the skeg provides the only lateral area beneath the water and is largely responsible for the board's behaviour. At high speeds particularly you can feel if it is well shaped and properly streamlined. The two forces involved are drag due to friction and a side force resulting from the motion of water particles in the waves. Both can be virtually eliminated if the skeg is correctly profiled.

Perfect symmetry and a sectional shape like a drop of water do not agree with the latest thoughts of American skeg experts. Mike Hynson of California believed he had found the perfect shape by copying, to a millimetre, the fin of a female dolphin in the Seaworld Aquarium.

A badly shaped skeg, or one with a rough surface, can vibrate at high speeds, just like a poorly streamlined daggerboard. Loose fastenings or the use of too flexible a material can also cause vibration, and the result is a reduction in speed.

The skeg has been the flash-point of discussions between American surfers for many years. Their main concern is to find the right compromise between the best possible directional stability, good lateral grip on the water and optimum turning ability when surfing across the front of a wave. It is the same when boardsailing without a daggerboard because, again, a balance between directional stability and turning ability is what is required.

The skeg has so far been sadly neglected by European sailboard designers and in consequence more and more sailboard owners are copying the American example by making their own skegs and fitting them to their boards.

Body dip and head dip

Playing games with the elements! Body dip and head dip are far from essential techniques but are fun to do.

To start with you go out sailing in spite of a strong wind. Then, as you improve, you gradually feel more at home on your board and no longer think of fresh winds as tiring, strength-sapping battles but as thoroughly enjoyable sport. You can play endless games with wind and waves. Two of these are known as 'body dip' and 'head dip' which, in spite of probably being the most useless things you can learn may well give you more fun than almost anything else in boardsailing.

For body dip you need a very strong wind. You pull the mast right over to windward and throw yourself back against the wind until your body touches the water and is enveloped in a rising cloud of spray. Then you lift yourself clear again to speed close above the water in a scorching plane. As you will realise body dip is not for those who are frightened of the water.

When sailing flat out on a beam reach simply bend your knees and hang right under the boom with your

backside fairly close to the rail of the board and just above the water. This brings your centre of gravity very low. A slight increase in wind can be countered simply by stretching your legs, pushing yourself further outboard, and at the same time keeping your arms straight. Try now to lower your body until it just touches the water and then sheet in the sail slightly with your sheet hand so that you are lifted again.

This introduction to body dip should be practised until the movements are perfect. If the wind eases slightly when you are hanging close above the water sheet in the sail firmly and simultaneously bend your knees fast to bring your centre of gravity as far back over the board as you can.

Knee thrust should also be practised repeatedly because you will in any case often need to use it when boardsailing in strong winds to avoid falling unintentionally to windward. Do not forget to sheet in the sail slightly at the same time as you bend your knees because it is the increased pressure of the wind thus caused that helps to lift you up.

Having practised enough to be sure of yourself you should have a try at

Body check slows the board and increased wind pressure on the sail pulls the boardsailor up out of the water. He can help this by sheeting in the sail for a moment and bending his knees.

full body dip. This acrobatic sequence of movements could also be called body-check because you hurl yourself into the wave in much the same way as you would try to bring down an opponent when playing ice hockey. Depending on how much you weigh you will need a wind blowing somewhere between force 4 and 6. Sail roughly on a beam reach, lower your body as described above into a wave trough and let yourself smack into the next wave crest. Sheet in the sail immediately so that the increase in wind pressure can lift you back to your normal sailing position. You will find that this is great fun, especially in warm weather. Another point, when your whole body smacks into the wave it acts like a brake and slows the board. The apparent wind suddenly shifts further aft, as you will remember having learnt, and pressure on the sail also increases.

You will find there is a limit because you can smack into the wave with so much force that you are literally torn off the board. When this happens you fall in to windward and can then try a 'water start' which is described in the next section.

Once you can body dip successfully you can try dipping rhythmically into every crest. After sheeting in the sail for a moment raise yourself slightly over the trough ready to throw yourself into the next crest. Raising and lowering yourself like this is a very good way of getting fit for long-distance boardsailing.

When it comes to head dip you only submerge your head and not your whole body. Just as for body dip you sail on a beam reach in a force 4–5 wind, leaning well out to windward. Instead of lowering your body close to the water you hollow your back as much as you can and drop your head right back so that you see the world behind you upside down— an extraordinary feeling at high speed. If you now bend your knees slightly your body is lowered until your head just touches the water.

In waves your head will, of course, be more deeply submerged and you will not be able to see for a short while. Remember therefore to check first that there are no dangers ahead. Nor can you see the set of your sail and this means that you will not be able to control it so well.

Should the board luff up sharply a fall to windward is unavoidable so, when sheeting in the sail, rake the mast forward slightly and you will then bear away a little when your head lifts clear. The board accelerates as it bears away and this helps you to regain your normal sailing position.

For head dip arch your back and bend your head backwards. This gives you a very unusual view of the water to windward!

The water start

This logical follow-up to body dip is not just for show but will be useful when it comes to racing. It is spectacular because you appear to be suddenly lifted out of the water again as if by an invisible hand after an unintentional fall to windward. A sharp tug on the boom, a squirm or two rather like those of a limbo dancer, and there you are back on the board screeching over the water.

How is it done? Obviously it takes a lot of practice and it is better to try in the warmest water available because, as is obvious from the name, most of your practising will be in the water. You will need a force 4 or 5 wind, depending on how much you weigh, because it is the wind pressure on the sail that has to lift you out of the water. A useful first exercise is to sail with the wind abeam or slightly abaft the beam, with both arms outstretched and gradually bend your knees, pulling the sail above you while you lower your body towards the water as if intending to do body dip.

When your backside touches the water do not try to get back onto the board by sheeting in the sail and bending your knees but submerge yourself further. This will brake board speed considerably, and you must take great care that your feet are not torn off the board.

So far this is virtually a deliberate slow-motion fall to windward. The board will have lost way in the meanwhile, and you are lying completely submerged with only your head sticking out of the water—obviously!—while your arms hold the sail pointing upwards at an angle and your feet are braced against the rail of the board. Your feet must be positioned correctly on the board because they must keep the board exactly beam on to the wind for a water start.

Push the boom up slightly so that wind pressure on the sail increases. It is often best to wait for a gust. Then bend your knees just as for knee thrust—in this case they will be under the water—to bring yourself nearer the rail of the board. This automatically raises the sail slightly higher and wind pressure increases further. Now you have to be very quick. Bring your knees above the board with a jerk, slipping your feet from the rail to the centre of the board as you do so. You should look as if you had bent right over backwards with your shoulders

Left: A water start. The sailboard is hardly moving and the principle is for the boardsailor to let himself be pulled on to his feet by the wind.

Right: A variant. The boardsailor allows himself to be towed along behind the moving board by the sail before pulling himself back onto the board.

nearly touching the floor. Simultaneously you sheet in the boom with a jerk so as to raise your body out of the water. If there is sufficient wind pressure at that moment you will have made a successful water start.

If the wind pressure is not quite enough wait in this position for a gust. If you then sheet in suddenly you will be raised as if you had been fired from a catapult. At the moment of lift-off bend your body forward because this will give the wind better leverage as it raises your body.

Preparing for a water start is like starting when water skiing where you also squat in the water before being raised by the motor boat's tow rope.

Do not forget to place your feet correctly when starting from the water. One should be forward of the mast foot where it can push to prevent the board from luffing up while you are being raised. The other is placed just aft of the daggerboard trunk and keeps the board balanced and beam on to the wind. The less you weigh the less wind is needed to start successfully from the water.

The waves should not be forgotten since they can be a great help when making a water start. If you let yourself be lifted by a crest the sail will be pointing up more steeply towards the sky and the board will benefit from the lift of the wave as you pull yourself onto it.

Remember that a water start is not simply an acrobatic feat. When racing it is far and away the best method of recovering quickly from an accidental fall to windward in a sudden lull, and you will be able to get under way again without losing any places.

Above: A closer look at the water start. Bend your knees and wait for a gust.

Surf-sailing

Of all the exciting experiences of boardsailing this must be the greatest, and brings a man closest to the elements. Surfsailing is both the reason why the sailboard was invented originally and the most advanced form of this sport. The power of the mighty waves of the open sea becomes visible when it is unleashed as the waves roll in unending succession to explode onto the beach with fearsome force. It seems impossible that a human being could survive such power with so fragile a craft and yet there are many photographs of people balancing on streamlined surfboards and speeding down the face of a giant wave just beneath the white foaming crest. Top boardsailors are now also able to surf-sail in these conditions and, obviously, they weigh the risks very carefully.

The word surfing is often used to describe the accelerated motion of a sailboard or sailing boat when it is swept along on the face of a breaking sea for some distance before sagging back into the trough behind the wave crest. To avoid confusion we will call this wave-riding. The word surfing will relate to the activities of a surfer using a surfboard (without a sail) in surf, and surf-sailing to a boardsailor using his sailboard in surf.

When you read the word surf do not immediately imagine immense waves 8 or 10 feet high. Wind waves are those, such as on inland waters and on the open sea, that form because wind blows over the water. True surf, on the other hand, is the zone of breakers near the shore where the ocean swell rolls in and breaks over the beach. Surf can be heavy or light depending on the offshore weather conditions.

The attraction of surf-sailing is not just the danger. It is far more a case of the thrill of speed when a fast-moving wave rushes the boardsailor along with it. Above all there is the enormous satisfaction of mastering the chaos of breaking waves and of sailing where you want to go instead of being thrown up on the shore by the power of the surf.

Quite apart from reliable gear, sure boardsailing technique and physical fitness you need courage, quick reactions and a cool head. You also need to know something of the dynamics of water in surf. Given proper caution and considerable practice every advanced boardsailor can dare to try his skill at boardsailing in surf 3–6 feet high.

First attempts should not be made in heavy surf. It is far better to try in light surf with a rather stronger wind. A sandy beach is essential: surfsailing off a rocky coast should be restricted to exceptional boardsailors only.

Before attempting to surf-sail you must be:

- Very competent in force 4–5 winds.
- Be able to keep your balance well in rough water.
- Be able to tack quickly.

The behaviour of waves

Wind raises waves on the surface of the water. The harder and longer that the wind blows from one direction, and the greater the distance over which it has blown the higher will the waves be. Other factors which affect wave formation are the depth of water, the shape of the bottom, currents and tidal streams. It is not the height of a wave, measured from crest to trough, that indicates its severity, but height related to wave length, measured between successive crests. The shorter the length the more awkward the wave. A 12 foot high wave, for example is much more difficult to deal with in the Baltic where its length will be about 90 feet than a wave of the same height in the North Sea with a length of 190–220 feet.

When the wind drops the waves continue for some time and may persist for 24 hours or more. But swell breaking on the shore in windless conditions can only be used for pure surfboarding. The rig must be left ashore.

Surf, then, consists of waves rolling up and breaking on a coast, whether it be steep cliffs or a flat beach.

Waves do not build up to great heights in the open sea because much of the accumulated energy is dissipated continuously when they break. The mass of water only appears to move forward. In reality it is just the

Once you have sailed in surf you are really hooked. The colossal power of the waves makes this *the* tremendous experience.

shape of the surface of the sea that alters unceasingly as the water rises at the crests and falls in the troughs. A floating object stays in the same place, moving up and down endlessly and, at most, may be blown slightly downwind. A long object always lies roughly across the direction in which the waves travel.

When considering the deep sea it is only the surface of the water that is disturbed to form waves. In stormy weather, for example, submarines submerge to find safety on the quiet depths. Where there are shoals and banks, and near the shore, the sea becomes shallower and the water particles, which follow a circular path in the deeper water, cannot swing down in a full circle. The rising sea bed forces the water upwards causing the waves to become higher and steeper until they break as surf thundering on the shore. Where there are off-lying sandbanks the waves rolling in break as surf much further offshore.

A thirteen foot breaker will hurl between 20 and 50 tons of water forward onto a beach near a boardsailor and, whereas the water in the ocean waves only appears to advance, the white streaks and patches of foam in the surf show how extremely fast the water actually moves near the shore. It runs far up the beach before sweeping back towards the open sea. It returns as undertow, which is a strong clutching current flowing seaward beneath the surface. Undertow has been fatal to many swimmers, especially where the beaches are wide and flat. It can even drag you out when you are standing in water that is hip deep.

Surfing and surf-sailing

This region of breaking surf is the playground of the surfer. With his surfboard he is carried forward by the wave and uses the wave's own forward motion. When he sees a large wave approaching from seaward he lies down and paddles to get his board at a slight angle to it, shifts his weight to allow the tail of his surfboard to be lifted high and keeps on sliding down the face of the wave. He balances the surfboard standing up and steers it with his feet. The wave itself is the sole source of power for the surfer but the boardsailor can make use of the wind was well.

To surf-sail you do not only need good surf and ample wind but, more important still, the wind should be blowing at the right angle to the surf which is from behind the surf at about 45° to it. It is only in the open sea that the waves move in much the same direction as that to which the wind blows. A sudden or even gradual change in wind direction only alters the direction of ocean waves slowly.

Hawaiian surf-sailing experts consider perfect conditions to be a force 5 wind with waves 11 feet high running at 45° or more to the wind.

Anyone attempting to surf-sail for the first time should at least have surmounted the force 4 hurdle and be confident when boardsailing in strong winds. This is what we mean when we talk about a surf-sailing beginner who must also understand the laws of motion of water in surf.

When working out to sea through surf each individual wave acts as a brake but when returning to the shore each wave accelerates your speed. They break in a regular pattern and you will need to find a relatively quiet patch through which you can sail seaward. When waves are high you need more wind so that the sail can provide enough drive for

Right: Showing the orbital motion of water particles in waves and the direction of water flow on the surface.

Below: A dangerous manoeuvre. This boardsailor is on the critical part of the wave which is just about to break.

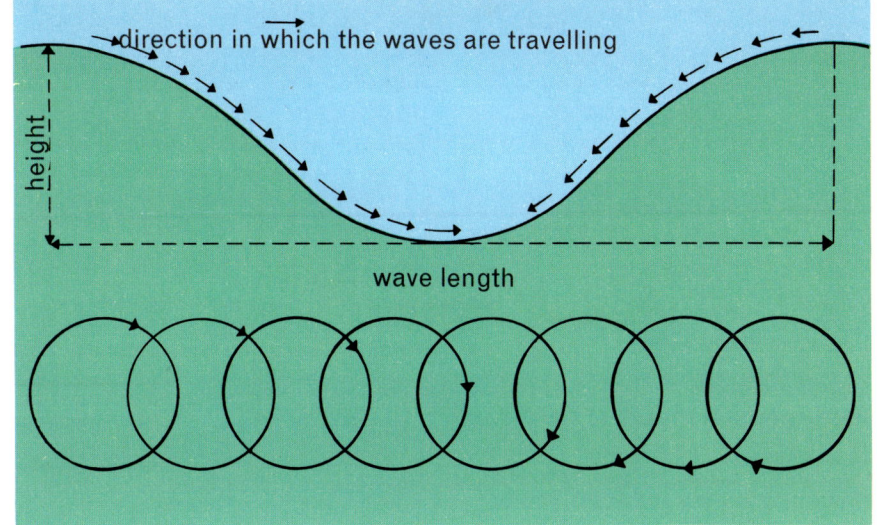

you to flee away from a dangerous crest.

The main difficulties when surf-sailing are as follows:

- To get offshore you first have to cross the zone of breakers.
- When returning to the shore you have to stay as close as you can to the breaking crest without being rolled over by it.
- You have to keep pace with the wave, in other words you cannot shoot straight down into the trough because of the danger of burying the nose under the wave ahead which would end your run.
- You must be in complete control when you sail into the area where broken water and streaks of fast-moving foam run ashore. The transition point is very abrupt and not unlike emerging from deep snow onto a smooth piste when skiing.

The surf-sailor has the advantage over the surfer in overcoming these difficulties because:

- He can balance himself against the rig thanks to the pressure of the wind on the sail, where as the surfer has nothing to help him keep his balance.
- He can use his rig to steer the board, whereas the surfer can only steer by using his toes and shifting his weight on the surfboard.
- By sheeting his sail in and out he can match his speed to that of the wave more easily.
- Getting offshore through the surf is less tiring. The surfer has no alternative but to paddle.

Surf-sailing in tidal waters

There is a special challenge to surf-sailing in areas where the tide ebbs and flows and it can be dangerous. Regardless of wind direction, in many areas the tidal streams set along the coast, first in one direction and then in the opposite direction, at a speed varying from hour to hour and from locality to locality. In some tidal waters the speed at which the tidal stream sets is negligible but in others its sets too fast to be ignored. It is therefore essential to find out about local tidal streams before setting out and, once you are out on the water, to check regularly to see how you are being set in relation to a landmark on shore such as a house, trees, an oddly shaped sand dune or rocks. Swimming gear left on the beach is invisible when you are offshore.

Never underestimate the effects of tidal streams and local peculiarities. In some river and harbour entrances, where enormous masses of water force their way through a narrow passage, the water can run up to six knots. If the wind is blowing in the same direction as the tidal stream is setting it may well be impossible to gain distance to windward, however skilful you are. Another problem is that wind blowing against a current

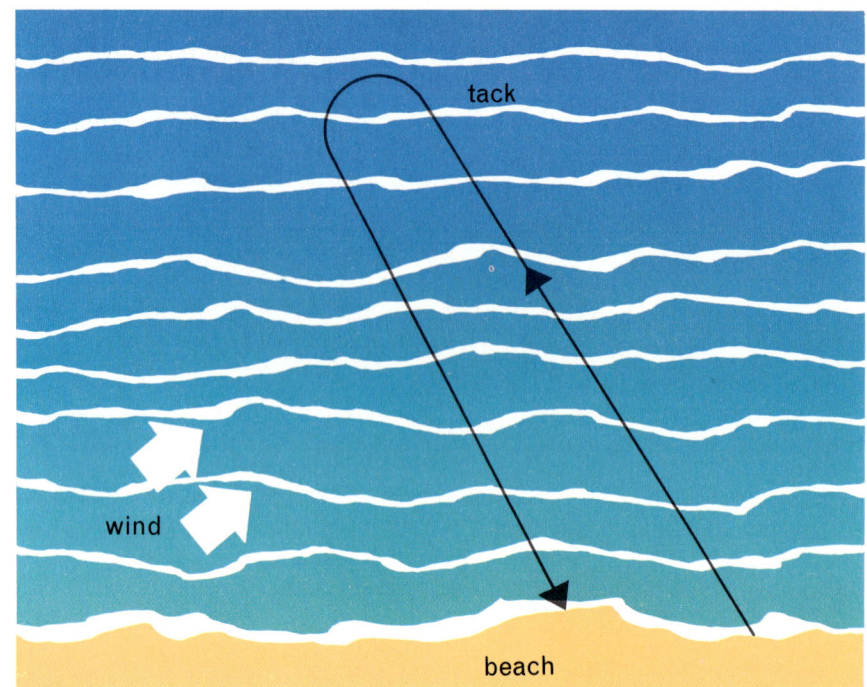

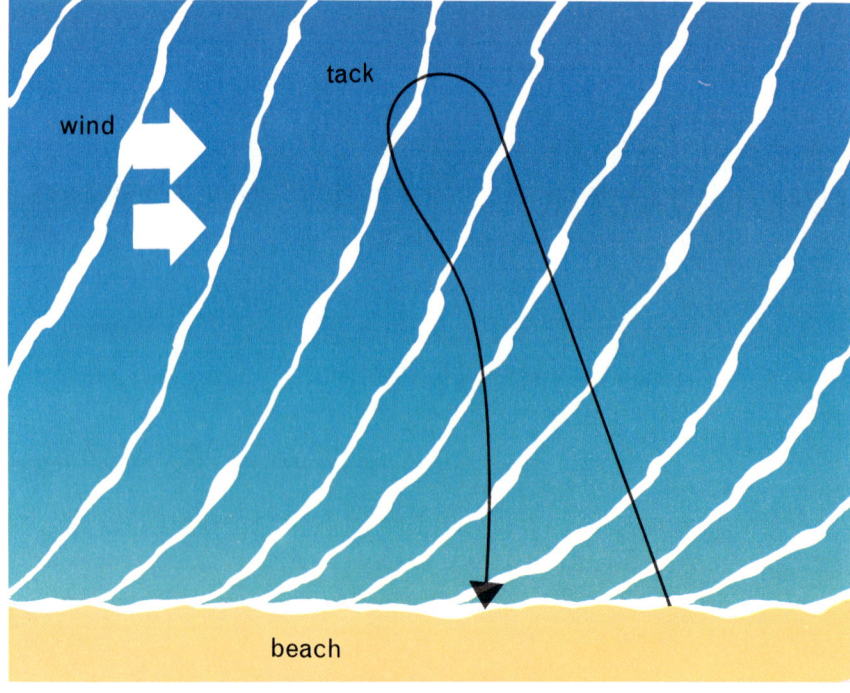

Top: It is only just possible to surf-sail. The board will be too close to the wind for fast sailing because the apparent wind will move too far ahead when surfing.

Bottom: The board will be close-hauled when working to seaward but can surf back on a broad reach.

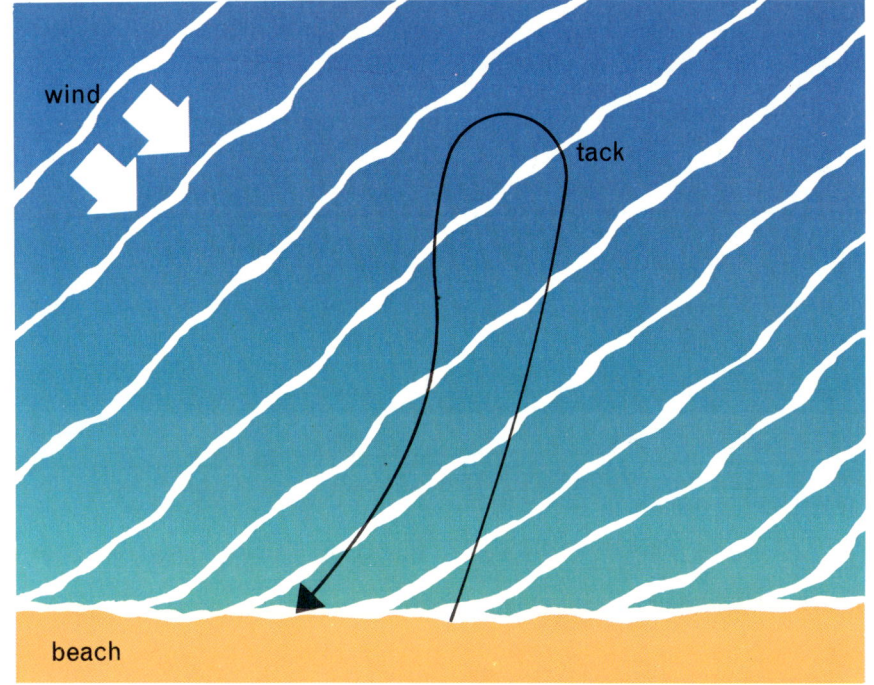

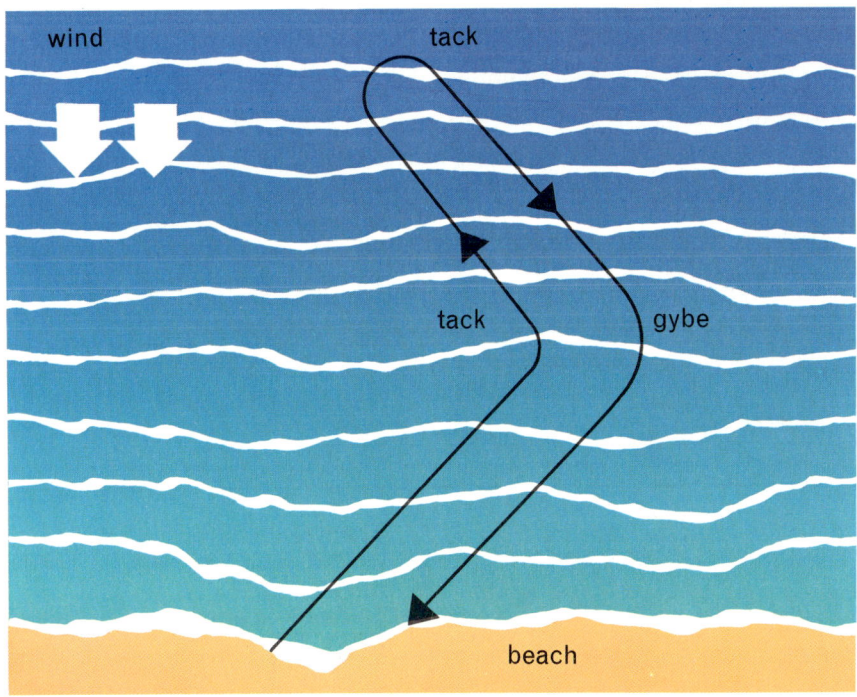

causes the waves to become steeper and to break. Wind with a current smooths out the waves. The former type of sea may be very difficult to sail through, though the current will at least carry you to windward.

The water is rough off seaward-facing beaches affected by tides. During the flood tide the surf becomes steeper and, where there are off-lying banks or shoals and where the sea bed is uneven, it may be so chaotic that it is very difficult or impossible to work out beyond the zone of breakers. Strong undertows and eddies occur during the ebb in the area of fast-moving streaks of foam. But apart from occasions when there is a dead offshore wind, boardsailors will find delightful surf, resulting from seas rolling in uninterruptedly from a great distance, along these offshore facing beaches.

The water off the inland-facing shores, for example off islands, is calmer and disturbed only by wind-raised seas but be careful, the tidal streams are almost very strong, especially in the narrows between islands.

Special equipment

Surf-sailing subjects gear to greater stresses than all other forms of boardsailing—and nowhere is the

Top: Ideal conditions for surfsailing with a broad reach back.

Bottom: Very difficult conditions. The board has to sail close-hauled out to sea against the wind and breaking surf and then surf-sails back on a difficult running course.

173

The surfers have paddled out laboriously and are now waiting for a wave but the boardsailor can sail through the surf relatively easily.

sailboard's simplicity better appreciated.

The surfboard has long been in existence, especially in Hawaii where surfing in earlier days was the sport of kings who were usually corpulent heavy-weights. They originally used just a strong mahogany plank, long, broad and heavy, with no skeg or keel. Today's surfboards are mostly plastic, some have very individual shapes and, most important, they have skegs. Sailboards are generally a patented design of a certain shape intended for use in all waters and surf by average boardsailors.

Long, narrow boards are least that long, narrow boards are least suitable for surf-sailing, especially if the bow is very low. They bore into waves too easily when sailing into the trough and overtaking the wave ahead. Most Hawaiian sail-surfing experts bend the noses of their boards up very high, just as the tip of a ski has to curve up to enable you to ski in deep snow.

Wooden or fibre-glass boards cannot of course be bent further after they have been made but it is possible to bend polyethylene boards which react to high temperatures. A possible method is to place the board upside down on a raised rack, warm the tip of the board with several infra-red lamps and shape it carefully by applying weights.

You can use solar heat on a hot sunny day instead of artificial lamps.

The tip should bend up no further than 8 ins, measured with the board laid flat on level ground.

Any board with sharp edged rails is dangerous. This could be owing to the seam of a GRP board being badly protected or to poor material having been used. At the very latest it will be after the first inevitable fall that the surfsailor's shins will appreciate the value of rubber guards.

Safety when surf-sailing

1. Always wear a wet suit, even when the wind is light. A novice surf-sailor is sure to fly into the water regularly, and the evaporation cools the body rapidly.
2. Use a safety strap to connect rig and board, but it is better not to attach it to the daggerboard because it would then be useless when you remove the daggerboard. Fit a small eye to the board forward of the mast.
3. The sail should not be stretched too flat, even in strong winds, because you also use it to help keep your balance which always needs plenty of power from the rig.
4. The mast foot must be held firmly in the step so as not to jump out every time a wave hits the board.
5. The outhaul should just be cleated on the boom without a knot tied in the end. You must be able to release it quickly before a wave can slam into the sail and perhaps break the mast.
6. Take a spare piece of rope with you, about 5 ft long, and attach it to the boom as a spare inhaul, outhaul or perhaps uphaul.

The boardsailor only has one more wave to overcome. It is breaking just ahead of him.

Working out through the breakers

Jim Drake and Hoyle Schweitzer's original object in designing the *Windsurfer* was to find an easier alternative to paddling laboriously out to sea when surfing. It is nevertheless difficult at first, even for an experienced boardsailor, to work his way out through the zone of surf.

Before starting off check the following points carefully:

- Are there stones, rocks or stakes beneath the water, or off-lying sandbanks and similar obstructions?
- Is there a quieter area where the waves barely break? How often do the occasional extra large waves roll in?
- At what frequency are groups of larger waves followed by groups of smaller waves?

These are factors which determine the right place from which to start and the right moment in relation the the rhythm of the surf. There are three alternative methods of getting under way: in the water, a racing start and an off-the-beach start.

Starting in the water

With this method the rig is raised and the board gets under way in the shallow water inshore of the breakers. With the mast stepped and daggerboard shipped the board is dragged into hip-deep water, one hand on the bow, the other on the uphaul.

You can face the surf or turn your back to it. If you have your back to it the whole rig will be floating in the water and it is not easy to hold both rig and board against the waves, especially when the surf is breaking over you and your gear.

In the smooth water of a wave

trough you climb on the board at lightning speed and raise the sail before the next wave breaks. The board has to be kept as nearly pointing into the wave as possible to avoid its being picked up sideways and carried back to the beach. Now you have to get sailing, and this is made more difficult by the speed of the foaming water and the power of the breakers which try to tear your feet off the board. You will understand why this method is possible only in moderate surf.

Alternatively you can walk out facing the surf with the board tilted on one side and the bow beneath one arm, holding the sail half raised and clear of the water by the uphaul—to leeward of course. This can only be done when there is a beam wind and it is really quite difficult to prevent the rig from trailing in the sea. When you are in deep enough water jump on the board, raise the rig fully and sail away.

Racing start

Speed is all-important when starting from the beach, so with this method the board is pushed into the water with the rig already raised and no time is wasted pulling the sail out of the water.

Far left: Starting in the water: With one hand holding the rig upright, he uses the other to push the board into the water.

Far right: The board is pushed through the first waves into water deep enough for the daggerboard to float clear.

Above left: The surf-sailor stands on the board, sheets in slightly, and is sailing over the first wave. The sail is still mostly shaking.

Above right: He now sheets in the sail and gathers speed as he sails through the second wave.

This is how it goes. Your sailboard lies on the beach absolutely ready to sail, the bow at the water's edge pointing seaward, the mast is stepped and the daggerboard is in the slot. Here, on the shore, you raise the rig and support it, not by the uphaul but by holding the mast above the boom. You will of course be standing to windward of the board.

You then push the stern of the board with your other hand to move the bow into the water, keeping it under complete control so that it stays as nearly pointing into the waves as possible to prevent the bow from being thrown to one side. It is vital that the sail should not touch the water and get caught. You then jump on board at the right moment in a wave trough and sail away as usual.

The right moment is when a group of smaller waves follows a large wave that has broken, but not where there is fast-moving foam or in tumbling foam. The trickiest moment is when you step on the board and before it has gathered way. Once you have learnt to survive this moment of uncertainty you will appreciate how the wind holds the rig while you push

Off the beach start

Top left: Set up the board and rig on the sand as if for a normal start at sea, but without dagger and skeg in place.

Top right: The wind fills the sail. The board may start to slide towards the water.

Bottom left: If not, jerk the board by bending the knees sharply.

Bottom right: Nearly afloat, the board starts to sail.

Right: Fully afloat the board sails off under perfect control.

the board into the water, and how clearly you can see the approaching breakers and so keep control.

Off-the-beach start

This is undoubtedly the neatest method of starting. A removable self-lifting skeg is essential and the daggerboard must be of a type that is inserted from above because the bottom of the board must be quite smooth with no projections. The wind must co-operate too—force 4 at least and preferably blowing from the shore but at least parallel to the beach. An off-the-beach start is just like getting under way as normal on a reach or a run, except that you start on the beach itself and are already moving forward when the board slips into the water. This is how it is done:

The board lies on the sand, fully rigged, with the bow pointing towards the water. Hang the daggerboard over one arm. The standing surface must be free of sand because of the risk of slipping so brush your feet clean when you step onto the board. Raise the rig as if you were standing on a simulator and prepare as for a normal reaching or running start with your front foot braced against the mast foot. Pull the sail aft and to windward past your trunk, and harden in with your sheet hand. The board, of course, is still lying on the sand. If you now bend your knees suddenly, enough weight will be taken off the board for it to respond to the pressure of the wind on the sail and it will slip forward.

If the beach is dry and steep the board may accelerate rapidly and shoot forward, but when it comes into contact with the water it brakes suddenly. You must be ready for this, bracing yourself firmly against the mast joint with your front foot an shifting your weight well aft. Otherwise you will certainly be jerked forward by the sail and catapulted into the water—yes, the well known catapult fall again?

When the board reaches the water or wet sand do not ease out the sail. It is only the board that is raked but the wind continues to act on the sail. If you deliberately throw your weight aft you can transmit this wind pressure by the leg braced against the mast foot to the board, so giving it a shove which thrusts it over the borderline. Jerky progress over the sand soon changes into a sliding phase and the board will sail fast as soon as it is fully afloat.

If the board is reluctant to shift from its position on the sand sheet in the sail and bend your knees sharply several times, or get a helper to give you a shove until it is freed.

Training shoes are absolutely essential for an off-the-beach start. you should also check carefully that the mast foot can release itself from the step. Adjust it at first so that the mast foot releases relatively easily.

An off-the-beach start is the answer when heavy, steep surf breaks very close to the water's edge. If you start from hip-deep water you may well manage to climb on to the board but the waves follow each other at such short intervals that the board is quickly turned away from the proper starting position head on to the waves and there is too little time to raise the sail in the short wave trough.

Surf-sailing against the waves

Working your way to seaward of the breakers calls for more than getting under way successfully. The violent motion of the waves makes high demands on your balance but this is one of the main attractions of surf-sailing. There are some basic rules:

- Always keep the board moving and maintain pressure on your sail because this is the only way you can steer.
- Always steer your board straight into the waves. Only then will it present the minimum of resistance to the approaching wave crest. Avoid being turned sideways by the wave but aim to climb to the next crest by taking the shortest path. You can only sail at an angle to the incoming waves when you become more expert.
- Keep your knees completely relaxed, just like a skier on a bumpy piste. Absorb the up and down motion of the waves with your legs as far as possible by bending your knees when climbing a wave and at the crest but straightening them when descending and in the trough.
- Avoid burying the nose under the waves by shifting your weight. The tip of the board should not be pressed when climbing, and the board will then rise more easily. On the crest you take a quick step forward to tilt the board downwards and to maintain speed, but immediately shift your weight aft again to stop the board diving into

the trough due to its speed. When a board buries its nose in a wave the speed drops sharply and the surf-sailor is almost inevitably catapulted forward.

- The sail should be sheeted in when climbing so that all the wind pressure can be converted into forward motion, thus taking the board up the slope. When descending the back of the wave ease out the sail slightly to slow the board which will in any case be sailing downhill.

Expert surf-sailors deliberately break these rules by thrusting the board forward off the crest of a wave at full speed and keeping their weight aft so that they literally jump off the top of the wave. It does not take much imagination to realise that you have to be pretty good to absorb the shock of landing in the wave trough.

Often you sail straight into a breaking crest, or the tumbling foam of a wave that has just broken, and this can bring you almost to a dead stop. The sail must then be sheeted out to absorb the shock, but only for a second because, in principle, you should keep the board moving and regain full way as quickly as possible.

Masses of water and foam can tear the surf-sailor's feet off the board. He crouches low and absorbs the shock by sheeting out the sail slightly for a brief moment.

Tacking against the waves

A surf-sailor must be capable of tacking quickly and surely in calm water. Speed is the trump card in rough seas and the jump tack is preferable to the step-round method. Duck and jet tacks are only suitable for smooth water owing to the difficulty of balancing and if used in surf would be pretty certain to cause even an expert boardsailor to fall.

The best moment to tack in surf is undoubtedly when the board is moving slowest and that is on the wave crest. The board can be turned quickly because the bow is clear of the water and it tends to luff anyway when it is climbing up the face of the wave. It is vital to tack quickly and to gather way again immediately.

Leaping off the waves

You can hardly believe your eyes when you see photographs like these. The boardsailor takes off and flies, with daggerboard and skeg absolutely clear of the water. He seems to defy the law of gravity. How is it done?

Well, you need waves of course, but not necessarily the high breakers found off the Hawaiian coast because you can jump wherever breaking surf is reasonably steep. The essential is that the wind should not be blowing in the same direction as that in which the waves are travelling but either at right angles to them or slightly offshore.

You start from the beach and reach out with the wind abeam or on

Leaping skywards from the wave-tops is only for ace boardsailors. Such jumps are not restricted to Hawaiian waters. Wherever there is surf a board can be made to jump like this.

a broad reach. Instead of sailing into the foam of a wave that has already broken you search out a wave that has built up steeply just at the edge of the zone of breakers. Quickly shift both feet aft to prevent the bow burying into the wave and sheet in with both hands to get full wind pressure in the sail.

Two factors now combine, the board's own speed of some 11 knots and the speed of the approaching wave which will be about 12 knots. When these are added your speed through the water is over 22 knots and that is enough to take off. You are only airborne briefly but it is a marvellous feeling. If you intend to stay on your board you must watch out because it tries to tilt to one side. You can generally keep your balance by just easing the sail slightly. Your legs have to absorb the shock of landing smoothly and you must pull the sail towards you firmly with both arms to counter the braking effect of hitting the water.

Foot straps

The Hawaiians have developed foot straps to help them keep the board under control in the air when jumping, and this is useful at other times too, not only when surfsailing. These look rather like water ski bindings and have a very similar function because they discourage your feet from slipping off the board at high speeds and enable you to control the force applied through your feet. These surf-bindings are nylon straps and can be attached by means of glass mat and resin to fibre-glass boards only.

Foot straps have several advantages; they solve the problem of a sure foothold; when tacking and gybing you can apply considerably more pressure forward or aft so speeding up the turn considerably; above all they enable you to keep the board absolutely straight at high speed and, as most experts know, a board that moves straight through the water sails even faster.

Another strong argument in favour of foot straps is that they hold the feet down and so make it easier for you to avoid a catapult fall. You will often have found that when a gust strikes suddenly your back foot lifts and you can only avoid a catapult fall with luck. With foot straps you do not get into this precarious situation because you can wedge yourself in beforehand. Designed originally for leaping off waves, this fitting therefore offers a number of benefits for normal strong wind boardsailors.

Waiting and resting

You can sit and rest safely on your board beyond the zone of breakers. Surfers do this too, not just to recover from the effort of paddling out but to study the waves and to wait for a particularly good wave on which to surf.

While waiting the boardsailor can relax his forearm muscles and cramped fingers. He can absorb the rhythm of the waves which seem to roll up in groups of seven, of which the innermost three are often the highest and, when they break, also the most dangerous. He can also watch his boardsailing friends coming out, a method of learning that is often underestimated. Quite apart from the safety aspect surf-sailing in company is more fun than sailing alone.

Most important of all you can regain your concentration and this is essential because when you surf-sail everything happens very fast.

While resting the wind generally blows the board to leeward so that the rig lies to windward and this is awkward because you then have to raise it to windward. It would take too long in waves to turn the board by the slow beginners' method and the board would probably be driven too close to the breaking surf. Best is to raise the sail when a wave crest rolls up, letting it pass beneath the sail so that the upper part emerges slightly from the water. The wind

Foot straps can be attached to the board so that the board can be better controlled when manoeuvring, as well as when jumping.

then fills part of the sail and, as the wave crest recedes, lifts the sail completely and slams it over the opposite side. You must react fast and jump over too.

Surf-sailing on the waves

The most thrilling experience of all for a boardsailor is surf-sailing with the waves. The sheer intoxication of speed, the battle with the elements, the spice of danger—such phrases only sketch a bare outline. It is hardly surprising that pure surfing has such an enormous attraction for both active surfers and spectators in areas where natural conditions make for good surf.

The great speed at which you sail in breaking surf is due both to the speed of advance of the waves themselves which sweep the board along, and to the board's own speed as it broad reaches fast with the wind free. A glance at the drawings on pages 172 and 173 shows that surf-sailing is possible when the wind is blowing in four different directions in relation to the surf. Up to the point where the wind is blowing from slightly offshore the boardsailor will be roughly on one of the courses shown. He will be close-hauled when sailing against the waves but will sail back to the shore on a fast reach.

Wave-riding on the front of a wave is worth while for a normal sailing boat provided that the wave is running faster than the boat can sail. The principal is always the same when you start, whether you are surfing, wave-riding or surf-sailing. Shift your weight forward to lift the stern so that the wave picks you up and carries your forward. If weight is not shifted far enough forward the board sticks on the crest and the wave just passes beneath it. Because board speed generally increases when wave-riding, the apparent wind shifts further forward and the sail therefore has to be sheeted in. It can even happen when you are surf-sailing that you speed so fast down the face of the wave that the wind due to forward motion cancels out the true wind. Take care—there is then no wind pressure on the sail to help you keep your balance!

A boardsailor generally planes faster than the wave travel. If he lets himself be carried by the wave he quickly finds himself in the trough and overtaking the wave ahead—so losing the effect of wave-riding. It is better therefore to increase the effective length of the wave by sailing down the face at an angle. You then have an endless slope to sail on for as long as the wave continues to roll in.

Now we come to the question of handling the board so that it keeps on riding the wave. Thanks to his sail the boardsailor has an enormous advantage over the surfer in that he can control his speed. This is now put to full use.

- If you are sailing too fast and look like rushing down into the trough and overtaking the next wave just apply the brakes by easing the sail out slightly so that you stay on the face of the wave.
- If you are sailing too slowly and it looks as if the wave crest will catch up and roll over you shift your weight forward and sail straight down the face at full speed with the sail sheeted in.
- Should your wave tower up fearsomely and start to break all you can do is to take flight by first sailing straight down the face and then breaking out to one side.

Surfers know well this game of staying as close beneath the breaking crest as possible. The ultimate ambition for the top Hawaiian boardsailor is to let himself be enclosed by water beneath the crest 'in a tube', and yet sail clear.

The normal surf-sailor must above all try to master the art of roller coasting by bearing away from the crest and then luffing up again. When sailing in he can of course let the wave carry him right up onto the beach but should he forget to pull up his daggerboard at the right moment his reward will be a mighty catapult fall as the dagger hits the beach. The daggerboard trunk can be split if he is not using a lifting centreboard or special short daggerboard.

If you take out the daggerboard in good time, running onto a sandy beach presents no problems because, even a rigid skeg will press easily into the sand. If you are really fit you can save yourself the tedious business of having to start off from the beach again after surfsailing in on a wave, by turning your board where the water is still deep enough. You luff up in the trough, speed along for a moment parallel to the wave and then turn towards the surf to sail out again. If you have to change tacks because of the wind direction you can tack in the quieter wave trough and then sail back against the waves and through the surf on the opposite tack.

But be careful of that carpet of fast-flowing foam near the beach! It can rip the board from beneath your feet. If you have to sail into turbulent foam do so at maximum speed. You may find it easier to sail slightly further towards the beach and then tack in quieter water.

The all-important rule for every surf-sailor is—safety first.

The ten safety rules for surf-sailing

1. Wear a wet suit.
2. Attach the rig to the board with a safety line.
3. The mast foot should sit firmly, but adjust it so that it can release.
4. Cleat the outhaul but do not tie a knot in the end.
5. Take spare rope.
6. In strong winds set a sail with enough camber (power).
7. Initially wear a life-jacket designed to support an unconscious person face upwards.
8. Sail in company; never surf-sail alone.
9. If the rig is damaged or blows away stay on your board and paddle. Do not swim.
10. Stop surf-sailing if the wind shifts to blow offshore.

No comment is needed to a picture like this!

Racing

Sooner or later almost every boardsailor goes racing, however small and unimportant the race may be by comparison with large events. He may later go on racing because he becomes fired with ambition, because he likes the sporting atmosphere during the race and the social atmosphere afterwards, or because he enjoys going to many new waters and meeting many more boardsailors. Here is a broad outline of the rules of the game to explain how a race is run.

Sailboards, like sailing boats, generally race in accordance with the *racing rules* laid down by the International Yacht Racing Union, plus additional *class rules* relating to the individual classes. These rules are supplemented by written *sailing instructions* which are drawn up by the race organisers specifically for the particular event and which are tailored to suit local conditions.

Whereas any racing sailor should have a thorough working knowledge of the racing rules and the class rules, because they remain the same wherever they race, the sailing instructions have to be studied carefully before each race. Quite frequently one of the racing rules is suspended or altered, and this has to be stated clearly in the sailing instructions.

We will begin with the start because, obviously, that is when the sailboards set off. The starting line is a purely imaginary line between two fixed points and your board has to be behind it when the starting signal is made. It can be very difficult to tell when you are on the wrong side of it. It may be marked in different ways, perhaps with a buoy at one end and, at the other, a mast or post on the

Left: The start line lies between a flag at far right and a point behind the camera. The starting signal is just about to be made.

Racing is another sport altogether but, for some, it adds to the pleasures of boardsailing. Racing calls for tactics as well as skill, no more so than during the congestion on the starting line. You need a cool head to come out on top when sailing in such close proximity to so many others.

committee vessel in which the race officers sit. The time of the start is advertised in the sailing instructions and is generally a fixed time. Sometimes, and especially in large international races, it is given as 'The race will be held after such and such a time at the discretion of the race officers'. The start can always be postponed by signal anyway.

Three starting signals are made, each being a visual signal accompanied by a sound signal. First comes the warning signal—the class signal is displayed together with a course

signal (key given in the sailing instructions) and a signal to show that marks are to be left to port (red flag) or starboard (green flag). Remember *Port* is *Left* and so, counter-clockwise; Starboard is the reverse. Exactly five minutes later the preparatory signal, code flag P, is broken out and finally, again exactly five minutes later, the starting signal is made by lowering both flags. The hectic chase begins—provided no *general recall* signal is made to start the whole process again—sometimes owing to too many boards being over the line before the signal.

Boardsailors are actually liable to the racing rules from the preparatory signal onwards and, as all the rules relating to the race operate from that moment on, any violation of a rule can lead to a *protest* and subsequent disqualification or other penalty. We cannot explain the rules in detail here. There are many complete guides on them as well as the Official Rules booklet itself. A few basic ideas follow:

- Starboard tack has right of way over port tack.
- A windward board must give way to a board approaching from leeward.
- An overtaking board keeps clear.

There are many other rules which cover specific situations. Amongst these, a boardsailor to leeward may *luff* and try to hit (and hence disqualify) a board to windward if the man on the windward board is astern of the mast of the leeward board. However, before the starting signal he may only luff up slowly and in such a way that the board to wind-

ward has room and opportunity to keep clear. Before the starting signal the leeward board may luff slowly until the windward board is head to wind, but this changes after the start when he can luff as he pleases but still only if his board's mast is ahead of the windward boardsailor. If the mast is astern, or has been astern, of the windward boardsailor he can only luff up to the *proper course*, which is normally the straight line track, to the next mark, or close-hauled, if the board is sailing to windward.

The rules about turning marks and *overlaps* which are mentioned later do not apply at the starting line but operate at all other marks of the course. An important point is that barging between the starting line buoy and a close-hauled board either shortly before or after the start is not permitted.

How to sail the course

Before starting a race the most important question is obviously, how is the course laid out.

A triangular course is generally used. The competitors have a 600–800 yard sail from the starting line to the windward mark which they round. A broad reach follows to the reaching mark either to the right or left, as specified in the course plan. The reaching mark will be about 400–600 yards from the windward mark and is rounded by gybing onto

Right: The triangular course has proved best for boardsailing too. A triangle is sailed first, followed by a 'sausage'.

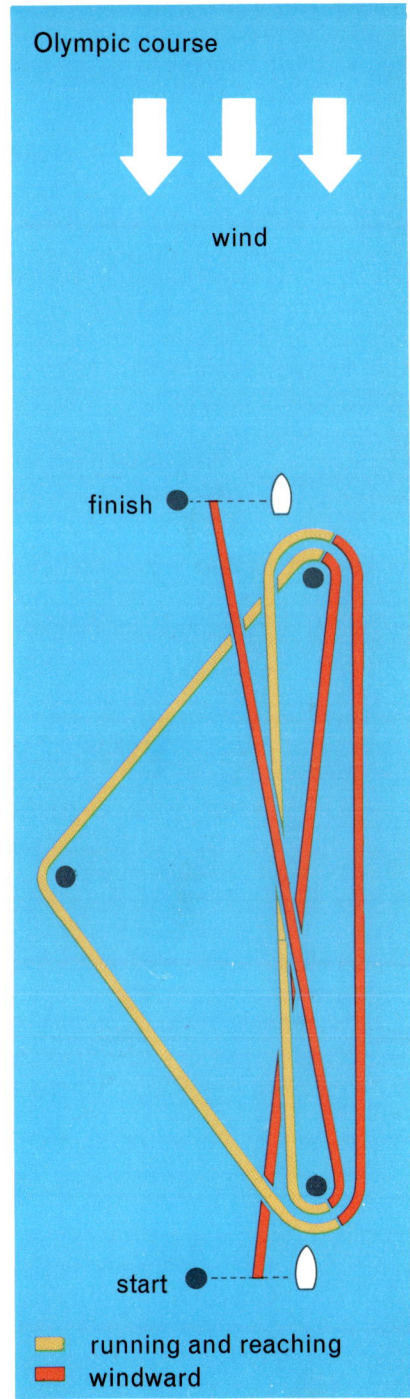

a second broad reach. This takes them back to the leeward mark which is usually one of the starting line limit marks. This, the first triangle, is followed by a second sail up and around the windward mark and a run back to the leeward mark. Finally there is another windward sail to the finishing line which is usually near the windward mark. Depending on the strength of the wind it takes between half an hour and one and a half hours to sail such a course.

The windward leg

Races are won to windward. This statement has been proved true hundreds of times. Just one bad tack can cost you ten or more places. After the start you need to sail clear of the bunch to avoid the wind shadow of sailboards ahead. Competitors to windward will blanket your sail and the wind you receive will of course then be disturbed and less strong than the clear, unimpeded wind.

You must therefore get your wind clear by sailing where other boards do not affect your wind. You can find a clear wind either by making a long tack to one side of the course, or by tacking repeatedly in clear spaces. Naturally you always have to comply with the racing rules and the most important rule is that starboard tack has right of way over port tack. On reaching the windward mark keep far enough away from it to avoid being forced onto it when rounding by an opponent or by a sudden shift in the wind. If you touch a mark you have to round it again—and that takes time.

The reaching leg

Now comes the fastest stretch of the race, particularly in strong winds, the leg down to the reaching mark. You can really get going, just as you normally do when sailing in fresh winds. Stay slightly to windward of the other sailboards if possible so that they cannot overtake you to windward and interfere with your wind. Should you sail so fast that you find yourself overtaking other sailboards to windward remember the third basic rule that overtaking boats must keep clear. If you touch an opponent with your sailboard he can *protest* and you can be disqualified from the race. As an alternative the rules may permit the 720° turn penalty for acknowledged errors. You

First board to cross the line at the starting signal has a clear wind and a good chance of winning.

Far right: On the beach at a world championships. This was taken in Sardinia at the Windsurfer Worlds in 1977.

then have to turn your board beneath you right round twice before sailing on, and that of course takes time and you will lose places.

At the reaching mark remember an important rule about the inside board. When within two board's lengths of the mark, the sailboard on the inside has right of way and must be given room to round the mark, provided that he *overlaps* his opponent. An overlap exists when the foremost end of one board lies ahead of a perpendicular to the aftermost end of another.

On the second broad reach you should again stay to windward of opponents to keep your wind clear. Should an opponent to leeward suddenly start to luff and you, as overtaking board, have not reached the point where you are ahead of his mast, he may well luff to force you away until he is almost head to wind. This is permitted under the *luffing* rule, but there is rarely much point in indulging in a private duel because, generally, the only people to benefit are other sailboards who storm past.

There are no major differences in rules relating to the second and third rounds. Of course all manner of racing tactics can be used when racing in sailing boats or sailboards, but it would be beyond the scope of this book to go into details. In any case the best way of learning is to race regularly. You will find that racing is great fun because the spice of competition and the use of tactics is added to the fascination of boardsailing itself. Quite apart from tactics you become very sensitive to wind shifts and the effects of tidal streams and currents.

Other types of competition

Team racing

Team racing is a fairly recent form of competition. Instead of an individual racing against other individuals one team fights against another team. Rather than sailing yourself into a winning position you have to think and fight with your team mates if you are to beat your opponents. A team race is not so much won by overtaking the opponent ahead as by covering the man behind and keeping him there. In other words it is the total position of the whole team that counts. Often the best move is to abandon your good position or the better tack and go to slow down an opponent so that one of your team mates can overtake both of you and thus gain two places overall.

A team consists of three boardsailors, and the best racing has often resulted when two are men and one a woman. Two teams race against each other round a triangular course which is usually of the Olympic type. Obviously team racing only becomes interesting when the teams are well matched. It is no fun if all three members of one team sail away into the blue. A race is more exciting to watch if spectators on the beach are kept informed of the position by loudspeaker.

Slalom racing needs an ability to tack and gybe with speed and accuracy. Technique must be perfect.

Slalom

The slalom is a variation of racing adapted from skiing by American boardsailors. Two rows of ten to fourteen buoys are laid, equally spaced and exactly in line with the wind direction.

When the starting signal goes two boardsailors have to sail to windward through the buoys, tacking round each in turn. When they reach the top they cross over to the other line of buoys and then run downwind, gybing round each buoy in turn. The first sailboard to get back to the start is the winner.

Parallel slaloms call for a great deal of agility and speed when tacking and gybing, and cause great excitement to spectators on land who can watch a direct battle between two sailbords.

Surf racing

Surf-sailing races are the most attractive alternative to the conventional triangular course races which sailboard classes first adopted. The zone of breaking surf is ideally suitable for racing sailboards because of their manoeuvrability and the simple way of sailing them. It is handling ability that counts. Advantages of weight and gear are not important if the boardsailor is physically fit, agile and has speedy reactions. Good balance, tactics and above all the ability to ride the waves are skills that almost anyone can acquire.

The fact that the natural conditions of a surf race in wind and waves may favour one man more than another is equally true of all other forms of racing. The boardsailor does not battle only against natural forces but against other boardsailors too. To be more exact, with the help of the wind and the surf he uses his technique and skills to beat his opponents. Surf racing is therefore only suitable for the few very good boardsailors.

There are hardly any rules as yet for this very new competitive sport, and certainly nothing so complicated or precise as the IYRU racing rules. The important points for surf races are:

1. Almost all sailboards in open classes may compete. Maximum length 12 ft 9 ins (3·90 m): Minimum beam 24 ins (0·60 m): Maximum sail area 64·5 sq ft (6·00 m²).
2. Other than essential safety regulations there are no unnecessary restrictions such as on using trapeze harness, taping the boom or using specially shaped daggerboards.
3. Severe conditions are sought deliberately, ie strong winds and heavy surf.
4. The course is laid out at the race committee's discretion. A testing course will include buoys in the zone of the surf as well as in the open sea.
5. Courses are relatively short, a number of short races being preferable to fewer but longer races.
6. The number of competitors is limited to a maximum of 25 if possible by running heats.
7. Start and finish are on the beach, not out on the water far away from spectators. In consequence starting technique and working out through the zone of the surf are extremely important.
8. The whole race can be seen and understood, even by non-sailors, because the short course is so near the shore.

The winner is the man who runs his board onto the beach first, and the overall winner is found from the results of a series of races.

Clearly the drama of surf racing is very different from that of normal racing and is much closer to the original idea of a contest. The success of a surf race obviously depends entirely on the weather conditions. Even if you choose an area where you know the surf is good there may be no waves on the day of the race and racing will then degenerate to a mere crawl, disappointing to spectators and boardsailors alike. On the other hand if the wind blows at near gale force every boardsailor feels the irresistible compulsion to conquer not only the power of nature but, above all, his own fears. Testing yourself to the limit is a large part of the fascination of surf-sailing.

The start of a surf race. The object is to work out offshore through the zone of breakers as fast as possible.

Buoy ball

This ball game for boardsailors was introduced at the World Championships in Sardinia and was much enjoyed by everybody. Buoy ball is a type of polo on sailboards and gives good boardsailors an opportunity to compete when the wind is light instead of squatting idly on the shore. Beginners become more skilful and learn to tack and gybe quicker when playing. You need eight like-minded people to make up two teams of four as well as an umpire.

This is how it goes. Both teams fight for a large red ball which must have a handle to hold it with. The area of play is bounded by three buoys, one to leeward where the game begins and two to windward which form the goal. There are two periods of play, 25 minutes each, with a ten minute break between them.

The umpire starts by tossing a coin on shore and the team that wins the call has possession first and starts the game. When the umpire's whistle goes one member of this team holds the ball in his hand or hangs it over his arm and sails round the leeward buoy. All the other players must at this time be in the area of play. The boardsailor in possession now tries to sail up to the goal as quickly as possible and, of course, his opponents try to prevent him doing so.

One way of taking the ball from him is to approach so close that you touch him with your board. Under the rules of the game he must then immediately put the ball on the water for the opponent to pick up. He may not then pass it to a team mate, which he could have done before being touched.

The opponent may only 'tackle' the man in possession when they are both on the same tack. If he is on the opposite tack he has to change tacks first before tackling him. To add spice the boardsailor has to keep his rig out of the water all the time. If the player in possession lets more than about 12% of his boom fall in the water, or if he falls in, he must put the ball down immediately.

When a player sails through the goal with the ball he earns five points for his team, but if he throws it through he only gets three points. The team with the higher total of points wins, and if there is a draw the umpire can allow extra time to be played.

The buoy-ball game. Two teams fight for the ball which has to be thrown or sailed through the two buoys which form the goal.

Freestyle boardsailing

An impressive trick. World champion Matt Schweitzer demonstrates how to rail-ride.

Freestyle, hot-dogging, or tricks are expressions taken from skiing, but acrobatics and tricks can be done as successfully on a sailboard as on two skis. It started in America, like everything else, where the Californian and Hawaiian coast boardsailors got tired of sailing normally all the time. They wanted to be able to do more, to improve control of their boards and to open up new dimensions for their sport. This led to freestyle. Performing tricks effortlessly gave pleasure and a feeling of achievement, even in light winds.

Enthusiasm spread from the USA to Europe where more and more freestyle competitions are now held each year. The object is to perform as many different tricks as possible and, as with ice skating, to assemble them into a programme. A jury then decides how many points to award to each competitor.

Freestyle is not restricted to competitions of course, and is most fun

Left: Tail sink. Getting the board vertical is a popular freestyle trick.

Above: It is easy to learn how to stand like this to leeward of the sail and it looks impressive.

when done just for show without being under pressure. Do not run away with the idea that such tricks are only for sailboard acrobats. Some of them are so easy that any relatively able boardsailor can master them with a little practice. A number of the best-known tricks performed today are described here, but do not let this limit your own inventiveness and so, work out your own new variations. A routine will usually include fast and jet tacks, running and stop gybes, body dip, head dip and water starts, all of which are skills that the keen strong wind boardsailor will have learnt anyway. But now some of the special freestyle tricks.

Sailing to leeward

This is exactly opposite to your normal way of sailing. Instead of pulling the sail towards you and to windward you stand on the lee side of the board and push the rig towards the wind. You can do this facing the sail or, as the experts prefer, lean back negligently against the boom to counter the pressure of the wind.

Inside the boom

This looks good and also saves effort. You stand inside the boom to windward and counter the wind pressure with your back instead of with your hands. You can also reverse this trick by turning round and facing the wind, holding the boom in front of you. Another variation is to stand inside the boom to leeward of the sail.

Boardsailing backwards

It is quite difficult to get under way backwards and to steer straight because the skeg keeps trying to force the board off course. It is therefore best to stand far enough forward on the bow of the board for the skeg to come clear of the water.

Helicopter or 360° turn

This starts with a stop gybe when you back the sail against the wind. Keep pushing and follow the sail round until the entire rig has turned a circle. Now sheet in and get under way again.

Above: It is more difficult to support the rig when facing to windward.

Pirouette

You can pirouette on your sailboard at any time, either by releasing the boom and spinning yourself right round very quickly or, in the case of the spin tack, by whirling round on the bow of the board while tacking. In either case you have to spin round extremely fast to be successful.

Rail-riding

The best boardsailing trick is to sail the board deliberately on its side, a trick invented by World Champion Robby Naish. You force the lee side of the board under the water and pull the windward rail up with your other foot. You can then stand or sit right on the edge, balancing by pulling the sail towards you. Real experts can ride the leeward rail too, rail side backwards and tack or gybe on the rail.

Below: How to get the rail up. One foot pushes the far side of the board down while the other pulls the near rail up.

Sailing lying down

We have already mentioned this in the section on running in strong winds. It is improved as a trick if you hang your feet over the boom.

Backwards Somersault

You will already know this jump, and you can well imagine that it can only be used as the successful conclusion to a sailboard routine!

Tandem Sailboards

Tandem boardsailing is not just a mechanical affair. The two crew have to co-operate and act in partnership.

One board, two men and two sails—this was the brain-child of Windglider designer Fred Osterman, and it caught on rapidly with keen boardsailors. Not only is it great fun to take the wind in your hands with a partner beside you but, up to now, the Tandem has proved itself to be the fastest sailboard. This is because it is almost twice as long as the one-man board and has twice the sail area. The only disadvantage is the problem of transport and storage because the Tandem is 22 ft (6·75 metres) long and weighs at least 110 lbs (50 kg).

How can you sail such a long board? You know already from sailing the one-man board that you sail straight ahead when the centre of effort lies exactly above the centre of lateral resistance because all the forces acting on the board are then in balance. But the Tandem has two sails, and the inevitable question that follows is—has it got two daggerboards as well? Of course not, because balance here results from the total force acting on both sails, and it

is the centre of effort of the two sails combined that has to lie directly above the centre of lateral resistance of the hull and the daggerboard together. The daggerboard is in the centre of the board, just as in the one-man board. Therefore, to keep the Tandem running straight, there has to be the same amount of wind pressure in both sails.

If the forward man eases his sail right out there will be no pressure on it and the board will luff up immediately because the force of the wind is only acting on the sail at the stern. This is why both people sailing a Tandem are responsible for steering. Broadly speaking the forward man luffs up by easing his sail while the man aft bears away when he eases out his sail.

The Tandem board can sail about 30% faster than the one-man sailboard.

Tacking with a Tandem.
Top: The man aft sheets in while the man forward eases out his sail.
Centre: The man aft rakes his rig and the forward man jumps round on to the opposite side.
Bottom: Then the forward man sheets in his sail and bears away while the man aft changes sides.

When it comes to tacking the forward man sheets out his sail while the man aft accelerates the turn by raking his rig aft. As soon as the board is head to wind the forward man crosses over to the other side and bears away on the new tack by sheeting in the sail. He may even back it slightly beyond the centreline. The aft man then also crosses forward of his mast and sheets in his sail. Similarly when bearing away onto a run the man aft eases out his sail while the man forward rakes his rig forward. A Tandem team has to work together well if the board is to tack and gybe quickly because one man cannot succeed without the other's help. The Tandem therefore is not just an aerodynamic unit but a partnership.

The 22 foot long Tandem is considerably more stable than the one-man sailboard.

Boardsailing on ice

No sooner had boardsailing started to invade Europe than enthusiasts invented a fascinating variant for the winter, boardsailing on ice.

First and foremost it is the incredible speed which can be reached that makes sailing on ice with a flexible rig so breathtaking. In force 4–5 winds an ice sailboard can reach about 50 mph (80 km/h) and that is faster than the wind. The best thing about it is the stability of the 'sled' as it flies over the ice thundering gently. The sailor has no need to worry about his balance and only has to concentrate on trimming his sail correctly.

Furthermore you can use any normal sailboard rig on ice and, therefore, all you have to do is to acquire or make the sled.

How does it all work? An ice sled is just a triangular wooden board with a skate under each corner. The two aft skates are sharp and keep the board straight, but the forward skate is rounded so that it can also slide sideways over the ice.

The mast foot recess, into which any mast foot will fit, is positioned so that the centre of effort lies exactly over the centre point between the rear skates. When the mast is raked forward the sled turns to leeward over

Ice board-sailing is most fun on clear ice. You can sail slightly faster than the wind when it blows at force 3.

Falling on ice is not too disastrous because you will slide but a crash helmet is advisable.

the forward skate and you bear away. Similarly the sled luffs up when the mast is raked aft.

The principle of steering is therefore just the same as on water, and an ice sailboard can similarly sail in any direction. You can even sail to windward better because you barely make leeway thanks to the sharp-edged skates at the back.

The only problem with ice sailboarding is the weather. It has to be cold enough to freeze the lake right over, and there should be as little snow on the ice as possible because wet snow, in particular, slows the sled down enormously. Thirdly a fairly strong wind is required because, depending on the weight of the sailor, the sled will only start to move in a wind of about force 2. It is rather rare to find all three requirements simultaneously in temperate latitudes.

But when you have a force 4–5 wind you reach incredible speeds. Tilo Riedel, inventor of the ice-sailboard, estimates that speeds up to over 60 mph (100 km/h) are possible, and the present ice sailing record is over 87 mph (140 km/h).

How is it possible to sail faster than the wind that drives you? Remember that a sailboard is driven by the apparent wind, and that this is the resultant of the true wind and the wind due to forward motion. Therefore the faster you sail the greater will be the component due to board speed and, consequently, the speed of the apparent wind increases with board speed. There is very little frictional resistance with an ice sailboard, and it reaches a high speed very quickly, so the wind due to board speed becomes the major propulsive factor. As a result you can sail with a true wind blowing from rather aft of the beam, with your sails sheeted in as for a close-hauled course, and sailing faster than the speed of the true wind.

The question arises whether such high speeds lead to appalling falls. You must wear a crash helmet of course, as well as tough ski clothes and good shoes, but the risk of injuring yourself is very slight when you are dressed like this because you are so close to the ice when you fall, and will just slide along until you come to a stop.

Boardsailing on land

It could be said that, when the boardsailor becomes too wet, he returns to the land. Some people have developed little trucks on rollers with a rig to be used on land on streets, runways, long beaches or even on grassy fields. Thus boardsailing has invaded the last of the surfaces of earth: first water, then ice and now dry land.

A basic difference must be pointed out first. Some land sailboards work on the skateboard principle. The mast foot is stepped on a type of skateboard and you steer with your feet, and not with the sail.

The second type is much nearer the principle of boardsaling on water and has a castor front wheel that can turn but is held pointing forward by a spring. This front wheel deflects the windward or leeward in response to a change in the position of the centre of effort of the sail, so that you actually use the rig to steer with. The main

The rather dangerous variant is boardsailing on land. Falls can do a lot of damage and cause injury.

advantage of the second type is that it is much more stable. It stays absolutely steady because the axles do not move like those of the 'Windskater'.

The major problem is that there are few suitable areas in which to sail, such as streets or long beaches where the wind blows in the right direction. Furthermore falls are extremely dangerous because severe grazes are all too likely unless you wrap yourself up in padded clothing.

Better than a skateboard. The balloon tyres enable you to sail on tracks or on the beach like a sandyacht.